NOTES

including
- *Introduction*
- *Characters*
- *Synopsis*
- *Summaries and Commentaries*
- *Medium: Verse and Prose*
- *Sixteenth-Century Political Theory*
- *Review Questions*
- *Selected Bibliography*

by
James K. Lowers, Ph.D.
Department of English
University of Hawaii

NEW EDITION

INCORPORATED

LINCOLN, NEBRASKA   68501

Editor	Consulting Editor
Gary Carey, M.A. *University of Colorado*	*James L. Roberts, Ph.D.* *Department of English* *University of Nebraska*

Cliffs Notes, Inc.   Lincoln, Nebraska

CONTENTS

This volume of Notes is based on the text in *The Complete Plays and Poems of William Shakespeare*, edited by W. A. Nielson and C. J. Hill (Boston: Houghton Mifflin, 1942).

King Henry IV, Part I Notes

INTRODUCTION

In the Stationers' Register, the official record of licensed booksellers and publishers in London, appeared the following entry for February 25, 1598:

> *The historye of Henry iiiith with his battaile of Shrews-burye against Henry Hottspurre of the Northe with the conceipted mirth of Sir John Ffalstoff.*

Later in the same year the First Quarto edition of the play was published, the title having been modified to read *the battell at Shrewsburie, betweene the King and Lord Henry Percie, sur-named Henrie Hotspur of the North. With the humorous conceits of Sir Iohn Falstlaffe.* Prior to the play's inclusion in the First Folio, 1623, five other quarto editions of the play were published. Among the ten chronicle-history plays written by Shake-speare, only *Richard III* provides comparable evidence of sustained popularity, both plays excelling in this respect all of the fifteen other Shakespearean dramas which were published in quarto editions during this period. *1 Henry IV* was and remains a favorite stage piece.

The reasons for its great popularity are not hard to find. The subtitle of the Stationers' entry and to the main title of the quarto points to the first and most important one: the *conceited mirth,* the *conceits,* that is, the jests, of one Sir John Falstaff. Not only is it that in this chronicle-history play for the first time comic scenes alternate with the serious ones, but in the portrayal of Sir John Falstaff, Shakespeare created the greatest comic character certainly in English literature and quite possibly in world liter-ature. And among all characters in drama this same Falstaff emerges as one of the most complex.

The reference to "Hotspur of the North" in both subtitles points to a second reason. Henry Percy, or Hotspur, emerges as the most prominent of the rebel leaders, an attractive if headstrong young man, one not devoid of heroic and tragic stature. The role of Hotspur in the main plot brings up the subject of structure. The typical chronicle-history play, of which Shakespeare's *Henry VI* plays are representative, tends to be epic in structure; that is, it tends to lack focus and to present action characterized by a series of climaxes prior to the resolution. The subtitles of *1 Henry IV* give some indication of what the dramatist has accomplished: this is a play about rebellion; the royal forces are pitted against rebels among whom Hotspur is pre-eminent. But in the play, although King Henry is the titular hero and does lead his forces against enemies of the Crown, it is his son and heir, Prince Hal (as he is called familiarly), who directly opposes Hotspur. In all likelihood influenced by his contemporary, Samuel Daniel, whose narrative history in verse, *The Civil Wars between the Two Houses of Lancaster and York*, Books I-IV, was published in 1595, Shakespeare made Hotspur the young contemporary of Prince Hal, although the rebel leader was actually somewhat older than Henry IV. The structural advantage of all this should be apparent. There is an admirable centralizing of the conflict as the action rises to its climax and falls to its resolution at Shrewsbury. Furthermore, Shakespeare compressed the historical action, which extended from June, 1402, to July, 1403, into a few months.

1 Henry IV ranks high among all of the thirty-seven plays in the Shakespeare canon for superior portrayal of characters, leading and subordinate. Brief notice has been made already to the prime example, Sir John Falstaff, who unquestionably disreputable, is endowed with such a superior wit in his comic revolt against law and order that some critics would elevate him to the status of hero. In important ways both Prince Hal and Hotspur are leading characters who are no less well realized, and much can be said for the characterizations of lesser figures, including Worcester, Glendower, and even Poins. In addition to these virtues, one should also consider the maturity of style, both in verse and in prose, a style notable for its wide range, vivid imagery, and strong verbs. Excepting only romantic love (found, for example, in that later chronicle-history play, Henry V), Henry IV gives us God's plenty.

For the main plot Shakespeare depended chiefly upon Holinshed's *The Chronicles of England, Scotland, and Ireland,* Vol. III, 1587, avoiding any change in sequence of historical events with the exception of that in which the king and Prince Hal achieve reconciliation (III.ii), which actually took place nearly ten years after the Battle of Shrewsbury. The way in which the dramatist selected and changed specific details to suit his purpose may be illustrated by the following quotation from Holinshed:

> The king, in deed, was raised, & did that daie manie a noble feat of armes for, as it is written, he slue that daie with his owne hands six and thirtie persons of his enimies. The other [Prince Hal] on his part, incouraged by his dooings, fought valiantlie, and slue the lord Persie, called sir Henrie Hotspurre.

In Shakespeare's play, it is Prince Hal, especially, who is accorded the laurels of the peerless warrior, refusing to retire from battle despite his wounds, rescuing his royal father from the renowned Douglas, and defeating Hotspur in single combat. King Henry, the titular hero, is not given comparable prominence in this culminating episode, although his kingly virtues are not ignored.

When this play was first produced, Falstaff was identified not by that name but as Sir John Oldcastle. Evidence of this original identification remains, for Prince Hal calls the fat knight "my old lad of the castle" in the first comic scene (I.ii.46). Moreover, in *2 Henry IV*, the 1599 quarto uses *Old.* for *Fal.* as one of the speech prefixes (I.ii.137) and the epilogue to *2 Henry IV* includes the statement that "Oldcastle died martyr, and this is not the man." The historical Sir John Oldcastle was a well-known aristocrat during the reign of Henry V, and a leader of the Lollards, that faction whose religious views were considered heretical, for which reason he ultimately was burned at the stake. Descendants of Oldcastle, the Lords Cobham, flourished in Protestant sixteenth-century England and understandably were offended by the use of their ancestor's name.

The historical Oldcastle received some notice in Holinshed's *Chronicles*, but that is not the source used by Shakespeare in this instance. He found the name in the anonymous *Famous Victories of Henry V*, a comedy-history play which was produced as early as 1588, but not published until a decade later. This excessively inept drama deserves brief attention as a second source used by Shakespeare, especially for the comic scenes in his play.

In *Famous Victories* Sir John Oldcastle, familiarly called "Jockey," plays a subordinate role. A comparison of him with Shakespeare's Falstaff is one of the surest ways of attaining a sound appreciation of our dramatist's creativity. But the playwright's debt, however slight, must be acknowledged here. This is also true of Hal's relationship with the habitués of the Boar's-Head Tavern and especially the robbery at Gadshill. Indeed, the confusing name Gadshill for one of the participants in the robbery derives from the earlier play, and in it Prince Hal is no more than an irresponsible, dissipated prodigal.

The name *Falstaff* may well derive from the Sir John Falstoffe, a historical figure, who makes a brief appearance in Shakespeare's *1 Henry VI* and who, according to many chronicles, was one-time owner of the Boar's-Head Tavern.

Historically, *1 Henry IV* continues the action set forth in Shakespeare's *The Tragedy of Richard II* (1595), and the dramatist necessarily includes in it many references to events dramatized in the earlier play. These include the events leading up to the usurpation of the throne by Bolingbroke (who thus became Henry IV), aided by the powerful baronial family of the Percies; the ominous prophecy of the fallen Richard, for whose death Bolingbroke was responsible; the new king's determination to do penance for his heinous crimes by fighting the enemies of Christendom in the Holy Land, once political matters in England are settled.

The Earl of Northumberland, as leader of the Percy faction, is quite prominent in *Richard II*, and his son Henry Percy, better known as Hotspur, is also among the *dramatis personae*. Hotspur describes himself as "tender, raw, and young" (II.iii.42); he fights courageously in behalf of Bolingbroke and is present at the deposition of the anointed monarch, Richard II. Young Prince Hal does not make an appearance in this earlier play, but in it he is set in opposition to the valiant Hotspur. Late in the action, the triumphant Bolingbroke asks, "Can no man tell me of my unthrifty son?" (V.iii.1). And he makes reference to Hal's "unrestrained loose companions," to the "dissolute crew" with whom the prince, "wanton" (carefree) and "effeminate" (refusing to accept manly responsibility), fraternizes. Thus the public characters of Hotspur and Hal are already well established. But, in *Richard II*, when Hotspur reports Hal's impudent reply to the news of his father's triumph, Bolingbroke replies,

> As dissolute as desperate; yet through both
> I see some sparks of better hope, which elder years
> May happily bring forth.   (V.iii.20-22)

In this way Shakespeare prepares the way for the full-length portrait of the prince who will emerge as the Ideal Prince, the leader who was to become the prototype of the Hero-King, the model of all English sovereigns, as he was depicted by all the chroniclers and as he appears in Shakespeare's own chronicle-history play.

CHARACTERS

King Henry IV

The eldest son of John of Gaunt, Duke of Lancaster, and grandson of Edward III, Henry had returned from banishment on July 4, 1399, to claim the rights of inheritance denied him by

Richard II. As these events were dramatized in Shakespeare's *Tragedy of Richard II*, he led a revolt against the Crown, forced Richard to abdicate, and became the first of the Lancastrian rulers of England; subsequently he had the hapless Richard put to death. In Shakespeare's *Richard II* and on occasion in *1 Henry IV*, he is referred to as Bolingbroke, from the place of his birth. History reports him as a brave, active, and temperate man who had been welcomed to the throne by all classes, pledging "to abandon the evil ways of Richard II" and to govern "by common counsel and consent." He is further described as being a good soldier, a careful administrator, and a wise statesman. Nevertheless, his position was insecure and trying because of the manner in which he attained kingship. Bitter experience was to make him somewhat suspicious and calculating.

Henry, Prince of Wales

Prince Hal, as he is usually called in this play, the high-spirited eldest son of Henry IV, had indeed been a carefree, boisterous youth, and the "wild prince" stories were circulated beginning in his own lifetime. History records also that he distinguished himself in the Welsh wars and gained valuable experience in government. Holinshed, Shakespeare's chief source, says: "Indeed he was youthfullie given, growen to audaucitie. . . . But yet. . . his behavior was not offensive or at least tending to the damage of anie bodie." That he did become alienated from his royal father is historical fact. Again in the words of Holinshed, "The king after expelled him out of his privie councell, banisht him the court, and made the duke of Clarence (his yoonger brother) president of the counsell in his steed." Reconciliation followed, but much later than in Shakespeare's play. In the *Henry IV* plays, the dramatist depicts the apparent waywardness of the prince and the profound concern of the king, both happily resolved by Hal's chivalry and heroism at Shrewsbury.

Henry Percy, surnamed Hotspur

Son of the Earl of Northumberland and nephew of the Earl of Worcester, Hotspur emerges as the impetuous leader of the northern rebels. Again it was Holinshed who provided the basic elements of his character; but it remained for Shakespeare to so develop that character, consistent with his purpose of providing a strong contrast primarily to Prince Hal and secondarily to King Henry, that the Hotspur of this play is almost an original creation. He is identified only as "Percy" in *Richard II;* in the present chronicle-history play, he is a major figure whose name suggests that he is indeed, in the words of Holinshed, "a capteine of high courage" spurring on the horse that carries him into battle.

Henry Percy, Earl of Northumberland

This is Hotspur's father, the titular head of the House of Percy, most powerful baronial family of the North Parts. He appears as he did in *Richard II* — cold and politic, in marked contrast to his son, a man who is, from the royalist point of view, certainly "a haughty, insulting" enemy of the Crown.

Thomas Percy, Earl of Worcester

Brother of the Earl of Northumberland and uncle of Hotspur, it is he who has especially influenced his impressionable young nephew. According to Holinshed, his "studie was ever . . . to procure malice, and set things in a broile." So he appears in this play.

Owen Glendower

First referred to as "the irregular and wild Glendower" (I.i.40), he was a Welsh nobleman, descended from Llewellyn, last of the Welsh kings. It was he who defeated and took captive Edmund Mortimer, Earl of March, who married one of Glendower's daughters. Incensed because Henry IV had not provided him redress against a grasping neighbor in a quarrel over landed property, Glendower led a great following of his countrymen against English rule. Traditionally certain supernatural powers were attributed to him.

Edmund Mortimer, Earl of March

Mortimer is presented in this play as the son-in-law of Glendower, the brother-in-law of Hotspur, and claimant to the throne of England. For the record, it was his nephew, a younger Edmund, who married Glendower's daughter and who, as son and proclaimed heir of Roger Mortimer, Earl of March, was claimant to the throne of England. By taking liberties with history here, Shakespeare magnified the dangers faced by Henry IV.

Prince John of Lancaster

Younger brother of Prince Hal, he appears in the very first scene and on the battlefield at Shrewsbury, where he is distinguished for his courage. To some extent he functions as a foil to his older brother, the Prince of Wales.

Archibald, Earl of Douglas

This "ever-valiant and approved Scot," as he is called by the Earl of Westmoreland (I.i.54) was a leader of the forces defeated by Hotspur at Holmedon. He then became an ally of the Percies in their revolt against Henry IV.

Sir John Falstaff

Knight of the realm, enormously fat and white-bearded, he is the companion of the carefree Prince Hal. Falstaff is concerned largely with pleasures of the flesh and cheerfully rejects conventional ideas and behavior especially suitable to his rank and age. He emerges as the most paradoxical character in all fiction, dramatic or non-dramatic. His irrepressible humor and superior wit, by means of which he retrieves himself from embarrassing or difficult situations, make it practically impossible for one to pass moral judgment on his character.

The Earl of Westmoreland

One of the noblemen who lead the king's army.

Sir Walter Blunt

Another nobleman loyal to King Henry and a commander of the royal forces at Shrewsbury. He functions especially as an emissary for the king.

Sir Richard Vernon

His role is exactly that of Sir Walter Blunt, but he serves the rebellious Percies, not the king.

Richard Scroop

The Archbishop of York and the ally of the Percies in the rebellion.

Sir Michael

A follower of the Archbishop of York.

Poins

Prince Hal's companion at Boar's-Head Tavern in East-cheap, it is he who devises the plot to gull Falstaff at Gadshill. His special relationship with Prince Hal suggests that he, in contrast to Peto and Bardolph, comes from a genteel family.

Gadshill, Peto, Bardolph

These three are the riotous and rascally associates of Falstaff. The first (whose name is identical with that of the scene of the robbery) serves as advance man among the rogues, the one who ascertains all the necessary facts relating to the planned robbery; the last named functions as a kind of parasitical serving man to Sir John Falstaff.

Lady Percy

Hotspur's sprightly, affectionate wife, she is the sister of Mortimer.

Lady Mortimer

Daughter of Glendower and wife of Mortimer, who dotes upon her. She speaks no English and her husband speaks no Welsh.

Mistress Quickly

This is the kindly, if rather stupid and disreputable, hostess of the Boar's-Head Tavern in Eastcheap.

SYNOPSIS

The main plot of *1 Henry IV* has as its subject the rebellion of the Percies, the northern baronial family who had helped Henry depose Richard II and attain the crown. They are joined by the Scottish Earl of Douglas, Edmund Mortimer, Earl of March, claimant to the throne, and Owen Glendower, a Welsh noble.

Henry is presented first as a ruler who has been beset with troubles from the start: civil strife in England, attacks by Scottish forces moving across the northern border, and the defeat and capture of the still loyal Mortimer by Glendower. He thus is unable to fulfill his earlier vow to lead a crusade to the Holy Land. But there is one piece of good news: English forces led by young Hotspur have defeated the Scots at Holmedon and have captured the renowned Earl of Douglas. Yet this especially gives the harassed king reason to lament the dereliction of his son and heir, Prince Henry, who sedulously has avoided the court and public responsibility and spends his time in the company of the elderly, high-spirited Sir John Falstaff, as well as the lowly habitués of the Boar's-Head Tavern in Eastcheap.

The comic subplot deals most amusingly with this same Falstaff and his boon companions, including Prince Hal, as he is appropriately called in this setting. In the initial episode, Hal joins with Poins, Bardolph, and Peto in a plan to gull Falstaff, contriving to have him participate in a robbery at Gadshill, be robbed in turn, and finally exposed as a coward and liar. Alone, Prince Hal soliloquizes, letting the audience know that, although he now chooses to enjoy himself in riotous company, he has no illusions about the character of his associates and will redeem himself publicly at the proper time.

The main plot takes precedence at this point. Once more at the court, King Henry confronts the Percies — Northumberland, Worcester, and Hotspur. He sternly rebukes them and especially demands to be told why the ranking Scottish prisoners taken by Hotspur have not been turned over to the Crown. The Percies, deeply resenting the fact that the man they helped to the throne now intends to enforce absolute obedience, begin to plot their revolt. They will make peace with Glendower and gain his support and that of Mortimer. Then, aided by Welsh and Scottish forces, the latter led by Douglas, they will war against the usurper, King Henry IV.

It is time to advance the comic subplot. Arrangements are completed for the robbery at Gadshill during the night. When the victims, a group of travelers, approach, Poins and the prince use an excuse to separate themselves from Falstaff and the others. Falstaff, forced to proceed on foot, is the leader of the robbers, who then are set upon by the disguised prince and Poins and robbed in turn. Falstaff exhibits almost miraculous alacrity in beating a retreat.

Again the action shifts to the main plot, wherein Hotspur is presented reading a letter from an English noble whose aid he has solicited. He can hardly contain himself as he reads the excuses offered and he denounces the writer as a coward. Then, in an exchange with his attractive young wife, Kate, he reveals himself as a man practically obsessed with matters relating solely to the planned revolt against the Crown.

In Eastcheap at the Boar's-Head Tavern, Falstaff is exposed as the dupe who has been tricked by the prince and Poins. But, not unexpectedly, in view of his already demonstrated wit, he not only survives the ordeal of being derided as a coward and liar but emerges comically triumphant. Prior to all this, Hal had made satiric reference to the prowess of Hotspur; now an emissary from the king informs Hal that he must appear at court promptly. This turn of events provides the prince the opportunity to participate with Falstaff in a "play extempore," each successively enacting the role of King Henry rebuking the wayward son and heir.

At the residence of the Archdeacon in North Wales, Hotspur, Worcester, Mortimer, and Glendower hold a parley, one not without some dissension. They plan the campaign against the royal forces and the later division of England into three parts. The absence of the Earl of Northumberland is significant in light of later events.

In the meantime, the confrontation between the king and Prince Hal takes place, the former sternly rebuking his son and comparing him unfavorably to the valiant Hotspur. But when Hal soberly vows to redeem his tarnished reputation at Hotspur's expense, the king not only forgives him but places him in command of royal forces. At that very moment the two learn that the rebels will be assembled at Shrewsbury.

Once more the action shifts to the Boar's-Head Tavern, where Falstaff is flourishing in the company of Bardolph and Mistress Quickly. The prince and Peto arrive, and we learn that Hal has reimbursed the travelers who had been robbed at Gadshill and has arranged for Falstaff's commissioning as a leader of the king's forces.

Hotspur, Worcester, and Douglas learn that the Earl of Northumberland and his retainers will not join them. Apparently illness has incapacitated him. Not for long is Hotspur dejected by this bad news; sure of victory, he sees this as providing a greater opportunity to impress the multitude, whose support the rebels must gain and retain. Vernon arrives with the news that the royal army has set forth for Shrewsbury and that second in command to the king himself is the Prince of Wales. Hotspur, at first depressed by Vernon's glowing description of Hal, quickly recovers himself and declares that he will oppose the prince in single combat. Yet a third report is received: Glendower will require fourteen days to raise a force of Welshmen. But nothing can dampen the ardor nor restrain the impetuosity of Hotspur.

Now we meet Falstaff as a military commander. Unscrupulously he has managed to enlist a group of pitiful, physically unfit "soldiers" whom he will lead to Shrewsbury. Both Prince Hal and Westmoreland remark on their unfitness but do nothing to stop Falstaff.

Sir Walter Blunt, emissary from King Henry, arrives in the rebel camp and addresses the rebel leaders, voicing the orthodox condemnation of their disloyalty and conveying to them the king's willingness to listen to their grievances. Hotspur restates the rebel's arguments, and the royal offer is rejected.

In Yorkshire, the Archbishop of York and one Sir Michael, both in sympathy with the rebellious Percies, discuss the impending battle at Shrewsbury. Learning that Mortimer and his battle forces will not be able to join the rebels, the archbishop expresses his deep concern for the success of the enterprise. He directs Sir Michael to leave at once to enlist support, for he knows that King Henry, aware of his disaffection, will move against him "if Lord Percy thrive not."

The action now moves to the king's camp at Shrewsbury. There, Worcester and Vernon meet with Henry IV, are given a chance once more to voice their grievances, are lectured on the subject of loyalty, and are offered generous terms if they will disband their forces. Prince Hal speaks words of praise for Hotspur, modestly concedes that he himself has been derelict, and offers to fight his rival in single combat. The two rebel leaders depart, ostensibly to report to Hotspur what has been said by the king and prince. Present during all this was Sir John Falstaff, who, left to himself, soliloquizes on the impractical aspects of heroism and honor.

Worcester does not tell his nephew about the king's offer, convinced that under any circumstances the older leaders of the revolt will be the objects of Henry's wrath. But Vernon reports honestly and clearly to Hotspur how Prince Hal conducted himself. When a messenger announces the approach of the royal forces, Hotspur sounds the call to battle.

In the course of that battle, Douglas slays Blunt, mistaking him for the king, and he exchanges words of warlike determination with Hotspur. A contrast is provided by Falstaff, who suddenly appears after the two have left. We learn that he has committed his tattered troops to battle, wherein they, with the exception of one or two, have been slaughtered. When the prince appears, deadly serious, Falstaff employs his verbal wit once more — and is sternly rebuked.

Prince Hal rescues his father from the sword of Douglas and meets and slays his great rival, Hotspur. After the prince's departure for another part of the battlefield, Falstaff reappears. Then, when Hal returns with his brother, Prince John of Lancaster, Falstaff claims to have slain the young rebel leader. Neither of the princes bothers to refute him at any length. Worcester and Vernon are captured and later put to death. But Douglas, also a captive, is set free by the generous Prince Hal. The rebel forces have been badly defeated. King Henry then dispatches John of Lancaster to the North, where he will oppose Northumberland and the Archbishop Scroop; he himself will leave with Prince Hal to fight the forces led by Glendower and Mortimer.

SUMMARIES AND COMMENTARIES

ACT I — SCENE 1

Summary

An exhausted King Henry describes the horrors of civil strife which his realm has endured during the twelve months that he has ruled England. At last he will be free to lead a united force of English soldiers to fight the enemies of Christendom in Jerusalem. But the Earl of Westmoreland brings news which forces the king to postpone this crusade. In Wales Mortimer's forces have been badly defeated by Glendower and Mortimer himself has been taken captive. Furthermore, English troops led by young Henry Percy, "the gallant Hotspur," are engaged in a battle at Holmedon against the Scots commanded by Douglas. The king has already learned the outcome of this battle, thanks to the services of Sir Walter Blunt. Young Percy has won a great victory and taken many prisoners. This is indeed, as Westmoreland states, "a conquest for a prince to boast of" (77). The king sadly replies that he wishes his own derelict son were more like the valiant Hotspur. He is concerned also because that admirable son of the Earl of Northumberland refuses to turn his prisoners over to the Crown, especially because many of them are ranking nobles. Westmoreland informs him that Hotspur's arrogance is the result of his uncle's influence: "This is his uncle's teaching; this is Worcester,/ Malevolent to you in all aspects. . . ." The king announces that he will hold council at Windsor and instructs Westmoreland to order the Percies to be present.

Commentary

The titular hero, King Henry IV, whom we meet and hear in his opening scene making what amounts to a formal address, had made the vow to fight the infidel in the Holy Land shortly after his usurpation of the throne from Richard II and the death of his predecessor for which Henry himself was responsible (*Richard II*, V.vi.30-52). Primarily, therefore, it is Henry, the sinner, the man guilty of the heinous sins of usurpation and regicide, who appears here — one who hopes to atone for his sins by going to the Holy Land. From a doctrinal point of view, never to be ignored in Shakespeare's chronicle-history plays, Henry is already enduring divine punishment, although, under God's authority, he rules England and merits the obedience of all subjects. This was the orthodox Tudor, sixteenth-century view which informs this play.

Understandably, then, King Henry appears "shaken [and] wan with care" (1), as he tells us in his speech, dwelling with vivid detail on the "furious close of civil butchery" (13). The rising of the Welsh led by Glendower points to the fact that Henry will not yet be given the opportunity to do penance for his sins. And with these internal troubles, there remains the threat from Scotland, still an independent kingdom. The seriousness of this threat is apparent: Sir Walter Blunt has ridden hard to bring the news of Hotspur's victory.

As he did in the last act of *Richard II*, Shakespeare now introduces the contrast between "young Harry," the king's eldest son and heir, and the dedicated, courageous Hotspur. The former's brow is stained with "riot and dishonour" (85); the latter is "the theme of Honour's tongue,/ Amongst a grove the very straightest plant" (81-82). Little wonder that the distraught Henry would like to exchange sons with the Earl of Northumberland, especially since Hotspur has been winning glory not in civil strife but in fighting a foreign enemy.

In view of the second reference to the postponement of the king's "holy purpose," that of leading a crusade to Jerusalem, it follows that the reported failure of the Prince of Wales is part of Henry's punishment for his sins. So Shakespeare's generation would conclude.

The titular hero has been introduced in this first scene, and we have gained an insight into one aspect of his character; the connection between this chronicle-history play and the preceding one has been indicated tacitly; and the dominant theme of rebellion has been established. Although neither Hotspur nor the Prince of Wales has made an appearance, the two have been set in opposition, and as a result the secondary but important theme of honor has been set forth.

ACT I – SCENE 2

Summary

The action now shifts to the Prince's apartment in London and the participants are Prince Hal himself, Sir John Falstaff and Poins. Prince Hal, far from engaging enemies of the Crown in armed combat, is amusing himself in witty verbal exchange with Falstaff. The subject of this discourse ranges from drinking to purse-snatching. The two vie with each other in trading amusing insults. Falstaff shows little deference for the prince, twitting him about his lack of grace and his devil-may-care attitude and behavior. Hal, whose initial speech provides a full-length portrait of the knight as a glutton and lecher who is too "fat-witted" to be concerned about the time of day, proves to be a rather worthy opponent in this combat of wits. But Falstaff matches him in rebuttal; indeed, some critics argue that the fat knight excels him.

Since the subject of robbery has been introduced prior to the arrival of Poins, the way has been prepared for details about the Gadshill enterprise in which Hal and Falstaff are asked to participate. Hal amuses himself at Falstaff's expense. First he refuses to go along with the others even "for recreation sake"; then, after listening to Falstaff's denunciation of him, he changes his mind; and finally he refuses once more to be one of the thieves at Gadshill. After Falstaff has departed, the prince learns from Poins that the robbery will provide a wonderful opportunity to gull Falstaff. Let Sir John, Bardolph, and Peto rob the travelers; then Hal and Poins, disguised, will rob the robbers. The great sport will be to expose Falstaff as a coward and liar. Prince Hal cannot resist such a good chance to trick his old companion; he will take part in the robbery at Gadshill.

All the dialogue so far has been in prose. Left alone, the prince now soliloquizes in blank verse. He makes it clear that he is fully aware of the character of his chosen companions, likening them to "contagious [poisonous] clouds." He states that he chooses for a time to remain in their riotous company for recreation's sake but will, at the right moment, surprise and gratify the world by standing forth in his true character.

Commentary

Appropriately, prose is the medium used in this first scene of the broadly comic subplot wherein matters of state have no immediate place. But one should note that, colloquial though it is predominantly, it is the prose of upper-class, sophisticated speakers. Occasional vulgarisms in the man-to-man exchange between Falstaff and Hal should not mislead the reader. Sir John here, and throughout the play, is a speaker of superior prose, prose marked by a vivacity, brilliance, and finish evidenced from the very beginning in his first two speeches with their balance, antitheses, and allusive elements. Hal, and even Poins, uses the same general style, which provides a significant contrast to that used, for example, by the lowly carriers in Act II, Scene i.

But most important in this scene are the characters of Falstaff and Prince Hal. What is learned about Falstaff as he exchanges spontaneous, good-natured insults with the prince? He is, to be sure, a knight of the realm, apparently a not unfitting associate of the prince, whom he meets now, not in a disreputable tavern but in the prince's London apartment. If, for the moment, we take literally what Hal says about him in his first speech (2-13), Falstaff emerges as one devoid of any sense of responsibility. Time, a symbol of the ordered life as used here, could not possibly concern one whose hours are spent largely in drinking sack (a strong sherry-type wine, especially popular in the days before gin and whiskey), overeating, and wasting half the day in sleep induced by gluttony. Add to all this Falstaff's alleged interest in bawds and houses of prostitution. Quite an indictment, and one which Falstaff does not refute: "Indeed, you come near me now, Hal," he replies (14). Yet he is anything but embarrassed. Is his way of life unknightly, ignoring as he does *noblesse oblige*, the obligations of rank? Well, let Hal remember that Falstaff "takes purses by moonlight" and thus does not follow "Phoebus, he, 'that wand'ring knight so fair' " (16-17). Here, demonstrating for the first of many times his upper-class learning, he provides a brilliant rhetorical commentary on gross reality and, as always, is fully aware of what he is doing. Moreover, only a superior wit could accomplish all this in such an adroit way, effectively answering what may well be a serious indictment of his character. Cheerfully, he adds to his offenses: he is one who engages in robbery by night and thus goes "by the moon," not by Phoebus the sun. The figurative language here admits to interesting interpretation relevant in a play, the main theme of which is rebellion.

Traditionally the sun is a common symbol of royalty; in this instance, it represents the king, who stands for law and order. Rhetorically and poetically, the moon may represent more than one thing; here it is unmistakably a symbol of instability, not only because it does not remain the same size to one's eyes as time passes, but because (as Hal points out) it governs the tides of the sea, which ebb and flow. One of the leaders of the Northern rebels of 1569, a later Earl of Northumberland, was denounced by loyalists as "the wavering moon." As a knight who follows the moon, then, Falstaff is a rebel (though a comic one) against law and order. And this conclusion finds support in his witty, elegant circumlocutions and epithets: when Hal becomes king—and Falstaff is always aware of Hal's status as heir apparent—let robbers be honored; let them be called "squires of the night's body, not "thieves of the day's beauty" (27-28). The opposition of day and night is that of order and disorder. "Diana's foresters, gentlemen of the shade, minions [favorites, darlings] of the moon," which is described as "noble [and] chaste," are other refined terms used by Falstaff to describe criminal activity.

When Hal's reply makes this very point, Sir John is quick to change the subject, or to try to do so. But the reference to the gallows and hanging, the usual punishment for robbery in Shakespeare's England, has been introduced by the young prince, who will not, for the moment, let his lively companion ignore it, thus the reference to the "buff jerkin" worn by sheriff's officers and to "durance," meaning not only "long lasting" but "imprisonment" (48-49). The culmination of Falstaff's rejection of law and order comes in his comic plea to the prince, urging him to have nothing to do with "old father antic [buffoon] the law" and to honor thieves, who are admirable men of "resolution" (65-70).

Hal obviously enjoys this repartee with Falstaff, who indeed is, as he will say later, not only witty in himself but the cause of wit in others. The young prince lays a verbal trap for the knight: as king he will not hang malefactors; Falstaff shall. Immediately Falstaff pictures himself as a learned judge—and then is told that, far from being elevated to the bench, he will function as the common hangman. Wit rescues him from this ignominious position, as he makes a play upon the word *suits* (petitions or solicitations made at court; suits of clothing). This is grim humor, appropriately like a jest on the gallows itself, for in Elizabethan times the hangman received the clothes of his victims and therefore was referred to ironically as the best-dressed man in England.

Wit or no wit, the subject of hanging is not a pleasant one, and Falstaff changes the subject and mood. He is "as melancholy as a gib cat or a lugg'd bear." And Hal matches him simile for simile. Falstaff's reply, "Thou hast the most unsavoury similes and art indeed the most comparative, rascalliest, sweet young Prince" (89-91), underscores at once his favored position as a kind of privileged jester and, surely, a genuine affection for the prince.

This by no means exhausts the facets of his complex character. Earlier (54-60), it was made clear that Falstaff willingly let the prince foot all the bills at the tavern. Now, having been matched by Hal in the combat of wits, he adopts another role. For the moment he becomes the penitent old sinner, acknowledging that he is "little better than one of the wicked." The style he adopts is that of the pulpit, biblical in its simple parallelisms and repetitions (95-98). How serious, how repentant he really is becomes clear at once. In mock sorrow, he, this white-bearded old man, attributes his moral downfall to young Prince Hal, whose use of biblical paraphrase in reply reveals his continued awareness of Falstaff's comic tricks.

But once more Sir John's ludicrous statement has made him vulnerable. When Hal suddenly asks, "Where shall we take a purse tomorrow, Jack?" (111), Falstaff responds with enthusiasm: "'Zounds, where thou wilt, lad; I'll make one." And yet once more his wit saves him when Hal dryly comments on this sudden shift from "praying to purse-taking": thieving is Falstaff's profession; is it not proverbial that the wise man should follow his own vocation?

When Poins arrives with the details relating to the proposed robbery, we learn more about Sir John. He declares that, if Hal does not join in the enterprise, Hal lacks honesty, manhood, and good fellowship; and that, in retaliation, Falstaff himself will be a traitor when the prince rules England. Ostensibly finding such virtue in thieves, Falstaff sustains the force of his earlier reference to robbers as "squires," "gentlemen," and "Diana's foresters." If one chooses to analyze this amusing reversal of values closely, it becomes apparent that Falstaff and all who willfully engage in robbery as a vocation are rebels against the Crown. Thus, much of the action in this comic subplot stands as a parody of the serious, public action in the main plot; moreover, the theme of rebellion is common to both. "Comic relief" will not suffice to describe the action in the subplot; there is much more.

Finally, as regards Falstaff, there is the question of cowardice, one much debated by commentators early and late in view of the knight's behavior later in the play. From Poins' remark made to Hal alone in order to persuade him to join in tricking Falstaff, one may conclude properly that cowards are not all of one piece. Peto and Bardolph are "true-bred cowards"; but Falstaff is a coward on principle, a practical realist, as it were, who will fight no longer than he sees reason (207-8). Nor will he prove to be an ordinary liar; he will tell the most "incomprehensible lies" about his experience at Gadshill.

How does Prince Hal appear in this scene? In popular tradition he is connected with various escapades including robbery; thus the early introduction of the theme of robbery would be immediately understood by Shakespeare's audiences. But the dramatist handles this subject carefully as far as the prince is concerned. It is Hal who is rather insistent in reminding Falstaff that thieves end up on the gallows. When asked to participate in the Gadshill robbery, the prince asks: "Who, I rob? I a thief? Not by my faith" (154). And we are to understand that he goes along only for the sake of duping Falstaff.

So amusing is Sir John that there is danger of underestimating Hal's wit. Falstaff indeed is the cause of wit in others, but time and again it is a remark made by the prince which provides Falstaff with the opportunity to scintillate. Surely one of the reasons that these two enjoy each other's company so much is that they share in the exhibition of verbal wit. For example, when Falstaff expresses his willingness to be hangman rather than judge because it "jumps with [his] humour as well as waiting in the court" (77-78), Hal gets the point immediately. "For obtaining of suits?" he asks. His last words addressed to the fat knight in this scene are brilliant: "Farewell, thou latter spring! Farewell. All-hallown summer!"

Prince Hal's final soliloquy has disturbed many readers. Some find it "priggish and hypocritical," and one may well conclude that it leaves the reader with an unflattering impression of Hal. Perhaps it is best here to remember that Shakespeare is dealing with a beloved, honored historical character whose youthful escapades and subsequent reformation had become part of treasured tradition. In a sense, the speaker is not Hal, Falstaff's "sweet wag," but Henry, Prince of Wales, who one day will lead English troops to victory over the traditional enemy, France. Here he functions as a kind of chorus. But once he gets beyond the indictment of his unprincipled associates as "contagious clouds" and "foul and ugly mists," his charm and breadth come through:

> If all the year were playing holidays,
> To sport would be as tedious as to work.
>
> (227-28)

These lines rescue him from the charge of calculation or hypocrisy.

Summary

A determined King Henry strongly reproves the Earls of Northumberland and Worcester, and Hotspur, who have obeyed his summons to appear before him. His threat to use force if necessary to curb their opposition leads Worcester to remind him that they, the Percies, were largely responsible for his rise to the throne. The king promptly orders Worcester to leave. Now it is Northumberland who addresses Henry IV, voicing words of conciliation. Hotspur, he states, has been maligned, for his son never intended to ignore a royal command. Hotspur himself explains what happened. Battle weary, he found it impossible to respond affirmatively to the request made by the king's messenger, a pretentious, unmanly coxcomb. Although the loyal Sir Walter Blunt puts in a good word for Hotspur, the king does not accept this excuse. He is convinced that young Percy intended to use the Scottish prisoners in bargaining with him for the ransom of Mortimer, Earl of March, Hotspur's brother-in-law, whom he denounces as one who foolishly betrayed the forces he led and now has married the daughter of his captor, "that great magician, damn'd Glendower." Hotspur vehemently defends Mortimer, but the king refuses to believe that he is not a traitor. Ordering Hotspur to talk no more of the Earl of March, he adds: "Send us your prisoners, or you'll hear of it." The king and members of his retinue leave.

Hotspur is beside himself. Even though he risks his life he will not obey King Henry. Just as Northumberland urges his son to control himself, Worcester returns to hear another outburst from his nephew. When Hotspur says that the king turned pale at the very mention of Mortimer's name, Worcester replies, "I cannot blame him." And this leads to a review of past events: Richard II's designation of the Earl of March as his heir to the throne, the role of the Percies in Bolingbroke's successful revolt, the ignominious position in which this proud and ungrateful Henry IV has placed the members of the House of Percy.

Worcester interrupts to announce that he has a plan, one "deep and dangerous," which he will reveal to his kinsmen. Hotspur is exhilarated by the very mention of a dangerous exploit to be carried out in the name of honor. Henceforth, he declares, he will dedicate himself solely to opposing "this Bolingbroke" and the Prince of Wales. Only after Northumberland has succeeded in calming his son can Worcester proceed. Hotspur is to pacify Henry IV for the time being by turning the prisoners over to the Crown, but he will make peace with Douglas and soon will ally himself with Glendower and Mortimer. Augmented by the Scottish and Welsh forces, the Percies will then confront the usurper Henry IV.

Commentary

The action in the main plot has risen to the point where the conflict is brought into the open. Following the audience with the king, the Percies are on the verge of rebellion. The danger to the Crown is very great indeed as Hotspur's speech beginning "Send Danger from the east unto the west" (195-97) makes clear. Henry faces not only the opposition of the most powerful baronial family in the North, but also, if the rebels' plan succeeds, the forces of Mortimer (legal heir to the throne according to the will made by Richard II) and the fearsome Glendower.

In this scene King Henry is represented not as the sinner, weary and wan with care, but as the forceful, competent ruler determined to maintain order within his kingdom as he faces baronial opposition. Yet he has been politic. The opening lines of his first speech tell us that he has sought to placate troublesome subjects, who nevertheless must respect him as one "mighty and to be fear'd" (6) if they prove recalcitrant. In the language of sixteenth-century political philosophy, Henry is a man gifted with the "specialty of rule." Nor does this conclusion rule out the fact that, in the words of Hotspur, he is a "subtle king,"—one capable of calculation, as a successful head of state has to be, at least in an era of power politics.

But this does not mean that Henry's crimes are to be forgotten. To Hotspur are assigned speeches which recall the sins of usurpation and regicide. For these the king and the Percies alike "wear the detested blot/ Of murderous subornation" and must suffer "a world of curses" (163-64). In counsel with his father and uncle, young Percy frequently disdains to refer to Henry as king; rather he is "cank'red [malignant] Bolingbroke," a thorn or canker in comparison to the lawfully anointed Richard II, "that sweet lovely rose." In the plant kingdom the rose is the appropriate symbol of royalty, just as the lion is in the animal kingdom.

All this may confuse the modern reader. Who actually is in the right, King Henry or the Percies, if either? The only way to answer this question is by recourse to Tudor political policy which, as has been stated earlier, informs this play. Henry remains a sinner; usurpation and regicide cannot be justified. But now a just God permits him to rule England. God may permit the rebel to rage as part of the punishment of a sinful ruler; but the rebel himself is guilty of mortal sin for his revolt against the Crown. A perceptive student may recall Richmond's leading a revolt against Richard III and emerging triumphant as Henry VII, first of the Tudor monarchs. Loyalists of the sixteenth century had an answer: Richmond (grandfather of Elizabeth I, ruler of England during the larger part of Shakespeare's lifetime) was the divinely appointed savior of the country and thus not a rebel. Perhaps it is well to remember that what most Englishmen cherished was stability—law and order within the kingdom. Richard II, in his latter years, was guilty of gross misrule; his successor, Henry IV, proved to be a strong, capable ruler.

Hotspur's basic character is firmly established in this scene. His high spirits and undoubted courage, his forthright answer to King Henry make him appear admirable. Unlike his uncle, the crafty Worcester, architect of the planned revolt, he is completely aboveboard. His sincerity is not to be questioned when he inveighs against "half-fac'd fellowships" (208) and the alleged ingratitude of the king. He is dedicated to winning new laurels in the only way he knows how; craft and selfish motive have no place in his character.

But Hotspur lives up to his name in more ways than one. Patience and contemplation are foreign to his nature; only in violent action is he at home. Time and again either his father or his uncle must rebuke him. Will he obey the king's order to relinquish the prisoners? "An if the devil come and roar for them,/ I will not send them," he exclaims (125-26). Northumberland's rebuke is hardly exaggerated: "What, drunk with choler?" No less revealing are Hotspur's words when Worcester first broaches his "deep and dangerous" plot: "O, the blood more stirs/ To rouse a lion than to start a hare!" (197-98). This Hotspur of the North is dedicated to winning honor after honor and now relishes the prospect of facing his major opponent, the king himself. Again it is his father's remark which provides telling comment on his son's limitations as a leader:

> Imagination of some great exploit
> Drives him beyond the bounds of patience.
>
> (199-200)

In martial affairs this young man is indeed the soul of courage; but he lacks discretion, he is too impetuous. Subsequent lines with reference to plucking "bright Honour from the pale-fac'd moon" emphasize once more Hotspur's special concern with honor as he conceives it (and about which, perhaps, he talks too much). In the words of his uncle:

> He apprehends a world of figures here,
> But not the form of what he should attend.
>
> (209-10)

To be noted also is that Hotspur is again pitted against "that same sword-and-buckler Prince of Wales," as he contemptuously calls Hal. By the end of this scene in which we learn that the Percies will be allied not only with Mortimer and Glendower but possibly with the disgruntled Archbishop of York, second-ranking churchman in England, Hotspur can hardly contain himself: "O, let the hours be short/ Till fields and blows and groans applaud our sport!" (301-2). His choice of the word *sport* referring to bloody conflict is as revealing as anything else as regards his character. Hal, we recall, has been manifesting a far different attitude toward what constitutes sport; and he is about to engage in an enterprise which is against law and order within the kingdom ruled by Henry IV.

ACT II – SCENE 1

Summary

Two carriers complain about the accommodations of the inn at Rochester as they prepare to drive their pack horses to the market in London. Gadshill, the professional thief to whom Poins had made reference, enters and asks to borrow their lantern, but the wary carriers refuse to lend it and leave. At Gadshill's call the chamberlain, an informer, appears. He confirms what he told Gadshill earlier: a franklin (middle-class landowner) with three hundred marks in gold will be among the travelers soon to depart from the inn. Unlike the chamberlain, Gadshill has no fear of the hangman because he is joined in the robbery by Sir John and, to paraphase his own words, persons of higher rank.

Commentary

The inn-yard setting is a little masterpiece of vivid writing. It is picturesque in the literal sense, evoking a memorable picture – the darkness of a winter's morning with Charles' Wain (the constellation of the Great Bear) visible over the chimney, and the flea-infested inn itself. The note of homely realism is enhanced by the reference to the death of Robin Ostler, his passing lamented by the lowly carriers, whose colloquial discourse provides an interesting contrast to that between Prince Hal and Falstaff. And all this has its place in a play, the theme of which is rebellion. The carriers are representative of a goodly proportion of the English people, going about their work in their unglamorous way. The quarrel between king and lords affects all Englishmen, including these carriers concerned about the comfort of their poor horses and getting their produce to market.

Gadshill, appropriately named after a stretch of road notorious for robberies, and the unscrupulous chamberlain provide the contrast to the hard-working, honest subjects of the Crown. Gadshill's speech is larded with the argot of the Elizabethan underworld; consider, for example, the references to "foot landrakers" (footpads), and "long-staff sixpenny strikers" (thieves who will bash a person on the head for a pittance). But more important is his reference to the exalted company who are to join him in the robbery; they are ones who

> pray continually to their saint, the commonwealth;
> or rather, not pray to her, but prey on her, for they ride
> up and down on her and make her their boots.
>
> (88-91)

His sardonic words unmistakably are applicable to the Percies with their plot against the commonwealth, represented by the king, just as they are to Falstaff and Prince Hal. One may well recall the words spoken by Henry IV at the beginning of this play. Speaking of the grave civil disturbances which have occurred in the commonwealth during the first year of his reign, he said:

> No more shall trenching war channel her fields,
> Nor bruise her flowerets with the armed hoofs
> Of hostile paces.
>
> (I. i. 7-9)

Again the thematic connection between main plot and subplot is made clear.

ACT II – SCENE 2

Summary

Prince Hal and Poins appear together on the highway near Gadshill. Poins has succeeded in depriving Falstaff of his horse, and the fat knight himself arrives calling for Poins, who has withdrawn into the darkness. Hal offers to find Poins, and Falstaff is left alone to complain about Poins' perfidy. When the prince returns, Sir John is no less voluble in his denunication of any one who would so "colt" (fool) him. When Hal refuses to serve as Falstaff's groom—that is, get his horse for him—the knight unrestrainedly and wittily excoriates him.

Gadshill, Bardolph, and Peto enter. The victims of these robbers are now coming down the hill; all must put on their masks and be ready for them. Prince Hal instructs all but Poins to confront the travelers in the narrow lane, while he and Poins wait farther down the hill, ready to waylay their victims if they escape the first encounter. Falstaff has a moment of trepidation but agrees to stand fast. Hal and Poins leave to put on the disguises which will serve their purpose later.

Rendered helpless, perhaps chiefly by the verbal explosions of Falstaff, the travelers are quickly robbed and bound. The thieves are about to share the loot when the disguised Hal and Poins set upon them. Bardolph and Peto take to their heels at once; Falstaff remains only to strike a blow or two and then runs off, leaving the loot. The thought of the corpulent Falstaff footing it all the way to London delights Hal and Poins.

Commentary

One may wonder how it happens that the travelers, including the well-heeled franklin, are not mounted and proceed afoot. Obviously, Shakespeare, actor and shareholder in his company, was the practical man of the theater; stage entries on horseback were impractical. Not only does he deprive the travelers of horses but capitalizes on this necessity by having Hal and Poins deprive Falstaff of his horse.

In this scene farcical action, the broadest type of comedy, is dominant: Falstaff is the victim of Prince Hal, aided by Poins, and is paying the price for his enormous girth and brave words, but Shakespeare does not permit him to become the object of derisive laughter. Again his lines are superb of their kind. Here especially he is the master of witty paradox. He will be "accurs'd to rob in that thief's company" (10); hourly during the past

34

twenty-two years he has vowed never to endure Poins' company
again. Yet he cannot bring himself to forego "the rogue's company." He calls down a plague upon all thieves who cannot be
true men. Paradox is carried even further. This corpulent old
man, for whom twenty-four feet up hilly ground is the equivalent
of seventy miles for any one of his companions, is the personifi-
cation of vitality when he confronts the travelers. His best line
is "What, ye knaves! young men must live" (95-96); here is the
Falstaff who, despite his advanced years and white beard, is the
very spirit of carefree youth.

From one point of view, Hal and Poins function as the wits
who so manipulate events that folly is exposed — specifically, the
folly of Sir John. But a serious crime *has* been committed, and it
is not easy to dismiss all this as no more than an escapade in
which the prince amuses himself prior to his promised reformation. For the time being, however, judgment must await the outcome of the gulling of Falstaff.

Some readers may be disturbed by Hal's refusal to show any
pity for Falstaff who "sweats to death,/ And lards the earth as
he walks along" (115-16). But that would be sheer sentimentality;
there is no occasion to conclude that Sir John is in great discom-
fort. He is enduring comic punishment, as it were, for his sin of
gluttony.

ACT II – SCENE 3

Summary

At Warkworth Castle, Hotspur reads a letter from a noble
whom he has asked to join in the rebellion. The noble advances
one excuse after another for declining the invitation. Young
Percy is indignant and scornful of the writer, who ignores the
fact that the Percies have powerful allies, some of whose forces
already have set forth for the place of assembly. Hotspur suspects that this timorous lord may betray the plot to the king.
Vehemently he expresses his defiance.

Lady Percy enters. She is deeply worried about her young husband, whose preoccupation with some serious business has made him neglect her and most normal activities. Hotspur will tell her nothing, and she suspects that he faces great danger. He does assure her, however, that she will join him at an unidentified destination.

Commentary

An occasional earlier commentator has argued that this scene may be justified largely on the grounds that we must be given a recess from Falstaff. This is a wholly unwarranted conclusion. First, the scene reveals the progress of the rebellion planned by the Percies in the first act; second, it adds appreciably to what is now becoming a full-length portrait of Hotspur, the "theme of Honour's tongue," as Henry IV called him at the beginning of the play.

Young Percy's choleric asides, filled with contemptuous epithets ("lack-brain" . . . "frosty-spirited rogue" . . . "dish of skim milk") are sufficiently revealing. In writing to the unidentified noble, Hotspur has eliminated any possibility of surprise; inevitably the king will be informed. Enraged to the point where he could "divide [himself] and go to buffets" (34), he nevertheless will brook no delay; he will set forth that very night, still convinced that the revolt is an "honourable" action. The figure of speech he uses to reassure himself is admirable: "out of this nettle, danger, we pluck this flower, safety" (9-10). Especially characteristic is his rough, yet good-natured, sparring with his wife. Declaring that this world is not one for playing with mammets (dolls) or tilting lips, he adds:

> We must have bloody noses and crack'd crowns,
> And pass them current too. God's me, my horse!
>
> (96-97)

It is hard to imagine anything that could be more revealing and graphic than Lady Percy's speech describing her husband's obsession with thoughts of armed conflict—a set speech, replete with rhetorical questions and balanced lines: "Of sallies . . . Of palisadoes . . . Of basilisks . . . Of prisoners' ransoms" (40-67).

But another side of Hotspur's character comes through strongly, one that is most attractive—a bluff manliness and wit of sorts. No one can doubt that he deeply loves his Kate, just as she dotes on him. His last words to her echo the well-known passage from the Book of Ruth and leave no room for doubt concerning the relationship between this attractive young couple: "Whither I go, thither shall you go too. . . ." There is irony in the fact that he will not tell her what the "heavy business" exactly is, since he indiscreetly wrote all about it to a fellow nobleman.

ACT II—SCENE 4

Summary

At the Boar's-Head Tavern, Prince Hal and Poins are entertaining themselves. Hal tells his companion that he has won much honor by being accepted as "sworn brother" to the lowly tavern servants. He engages Francis, one of them, in a bewildering game with Poins' help. First the prince, then Poins, calls for poor Francis, who, striving to please both, runs up and down stairs in a ridiculous manner, answering each call with "Anon [at once], sir." Hal makes the newly-arrived Falstaff and the rest of the thieves wait at the door while he comments on the significance of Francis' behavior, curiously shifting to a comparison of himself with "the Hotspur of the North."

Falstaff and his companions enter, the fat knight complaining bitterly about the prevalence of cowardice and calling for sack. He then tells how courageously he fought at Gadshill against enemies who, first said to number one hundred, are successively reduced to six or seven; and, as he testifies, two particular ones in buckram suits become successively four, seven, nine, and finally eleven. Hal and Falstaff exchange derogatory epithets. At last the prince gives the true account of what happened and challenges Falstaff to explain away the fact that he has proved himself to be a coward and liar. Falstaff, in his special way, does exactly that. Valiant though he is, never would he be one to kill the heir-apparent whom he recognized immediately by instinct. His spirits are uplifted, for he now knows that

Hal has the money taken from the travelers. Let all be merry, he exclaims and suggests a "play extempore"—a bit of amateur play acting—as a source of amusement.

A messenger from the king is announced. At Hal's request Falstaff leaves to "send him packing." During Sir John's absence Bardolph and Peto tell how the old knight coached them to back up his preposterous story. When Falstaff returns with news of the revolt of the Percies, the prince seems almost totally unconcerned. The names of renowned Hotspur ("that same mad fellow of the North," as Falstaff calls him), Mortimer, Douglas, "that devil Glendower" leave him unperturbed; unlike Sir John, he cannot be a coward.

But Hal must appear before his royal father, and this provides the subject for the play extempore, a kind of rehearsal, in which the prince and Falstaff play alternate roles.

The arrival of the sheriff and "all the watch" at the tavern door interrupts this merriment. At Hal's request, Falstaff hides behind the arras and the others go upstairs, leaving the prince with Peto to face the law. The carrier who accompanies the sheriff into the tavern identifies one of the thieves as a gross fat man—"as fat as butter." Hal assures them that the man is not present and that he will answer personally for any charges made.

After the sheriff and the carrier have left, Falstaff is discovered fast asleep and snoring behind the arras. "Search his pockets," says Hal to Peto, who finds only a tavern bill for a bit of food and vast quantities of sack. On inspiration Hal decides to pester Falstaff by giving him a command of foot troops which he will have to lead against the rebels. Hal himself will report to his father in the morning and will see that the stolen money is returned.

Commentary

This scene of broad comedy is at once one of the most hilarious in all literature and also one of the most significant in this play. No reader will want to miss any part of the fun; but no careful reader should be so carried away by Falstaff's superb performance as to miss the ideas relating to the theme and to the characterizations.

First to be explained is the import of Hal's remarks about his relationship with the tavern tapsters and apprentices, to whom he refers as "loggerheads" (blockheads) and "a leash (a pack, as of leashed animals) of drawers." To many, this episode hardly reflects favorably upon the character of Prince Hal, particularly the trick played upon the lowly Francis. Perhaps Hal's exploits with the drawers may be considered "miserable attempts at mirth" introduced "to show the quality of the prince's wit when unsustained by Falstaff's," the whole comprising "a very strange incoherent rhapsody" best explained by the prince's volatile nature and by the fact that he has "spent several hours drinking with the drawers." This is the view taken by an early commentator (*New Variorum*). More recent Shakespearean critics have taken a far different view and have found coherence and relevance in this episode.

In our century of the common man and with the prevailing tendency to create Shakespeare in our own image, it is easy to go astray here. For one thing, contemporary sources tell us that the gallants in Renaissance England took a sort of pride in being on quite familiar terms with drawers and that only favored guests were invited to the cellar to sample the wine in the hogsheads. Democratic sentiments must not mislead us. The prince of Shakespeare's *Henry IV* is at the highest rung of the ladder in a hierarchical society; in contrast, the drawers, worthy subjects of the Crown, are at the lowest rung. Yet Hal has won their admiration and affection, and they compare him favorably to Falstaff, that "proud Jack." In so conducting himself he has "sounded the very base string of humility." This could well be the best way to prepare for the day when he will rule all the people of England, all levels of society. In a word, in the first part of this comic scene, we are given an insight into the education of the prince, one who will lead an English army to France and be able to move freely among his soldiers on the eve of the decisive battle of Harfleur, listening to and understanding their conversation. From this point of view, Prince Hal has won a certain kind of victory. In 2 *Henry IV*, the Earl of Warwick, seeking to console the dying King Henry IV, who again has great reason to worry about his son's behavior, has this to say:

> My gracious lord, you look beyond him quite.
> The Prince but studies his companions
> Like a strange tongue, wherein, to gain the language,
> 'Tis needful that the most modest word
> Be looked upon and learned.
>
> (IV.iv.67-71)

As Hal explains to Poins, the trick played on Francis is a "precedent" (36), or example, one in which he has proved himself to be a man of "all humours." That is to say, he is willing to indulge himself in all the varieties of life, including the present kind of merriment. His devastating burlesque of Hotspur (114-25) logically follows. Young Percy, according to Hal, is like Francis in his concentration on one narrow field of human activity, for Hotspur is obsessed by thoughts of carnage in battle — with "crack'd crowns and bloody noses." Indeed, there is much special pleading here; Hal has been and still is a truant from noble exercises. He has yet to prove himself and to make good the promise he made at the end of Act I, Scene ii. Virtue must manifest itself in positive action.

To compare Hal's wit with that of Falstaff in this scene, or elsewhere in the play for that matter, is wholly irrelevant. Whatever Falstaff's limitations may be, no one can deny him pre-eminence in the realm of wit.

Falstaff is in rare form as he enters, denouncing Hal and Poins as cowards and identifying himself as one endowed with true "manhood," as one of the few "good" men left in a bad world. He manifests again his constant awareness of Hal's status as heir-apparent and his own status as privileged jester by declaring his intent to beat Hal out of his kingdom with a wooden dagger and drive Hal's subjects before him like a flock of geese —

including, to be sure, the lowly ones whom Hal has just been winning over.

When Sir John brazenly denies that he has had a single drink, although we have seen him quaff a cup of sack almost as soon as he entered the tavern, the way is prepared for his gargantuan lies concerning the number of assailants at Gadshill. His immediate reply to Hal, who points out that Falstaff's lips are still wet with wine (170), provides a key to the old knight's tall stories: "All's one for that" (What difference does it make?). Surely it is futile to waste one's time debating whether or not Falstaff expects Hal and Poins to believe him. He remains the great wit at his calling; exaggeration, as is apparent here, can be wonderfully amusing.

And so when, with assumed solemnity, he justifies his conduct at Gadshill, having been exposed as a liar and coward. As Hal knows, he is "as valiant as Hercules; but beware instinct: the lion will not touch the true prince." In identifying himself with the great exemplar of strength and courage in classical mythology, and with the lion (a symbol here, not of royalty, but of courage and ferocity in the animal kingdom), Falstaff illustrates another aspect of his complex character. Here he is the braggart warrior, a well-known type character in classical comedy, long since naturalized in Renaissance European drama, including English. But let us give Falstaff credit; he is aware of the full import of his words.

The nobleman at the door, an emissary from the king, is dismissed by Falstaff as "Old Gravity"; the elderly, white-bearded knight in whose life seriousness has no place is glad to "send him packing" (328). The epithet Falstaff uses here is at one with "old father antic," which he used earlier to describe the law. The implication is the same: he has no use for responsibility, for law, for order. They interfere with life conceived as a perpetual holiday.

There follows an exchange between Hal and Bardolph and then between the prince and Falstaff; these have some special interest in the realm of the comedy of physical appearances (340-60) and also have some thematic relevance. Bardolph's flaming nose invites Hal's witty comment; it provides a constant glow which should have served Bardolph as well as his sword during the Gadshill robbery, and yet Bardolph ran away. Perhaps, in contrast to Falstaff's undisturbed good humor, there is rancor in Bardolph's reply: "My lord, do you see these meteors? Do you behold these exhalations?" (351-52). But Shakespeare is making a typical play on words here. On one level, meteors and exhalations stand for drunkenness and poverty; on a second level, not to be ignored in a play about rebellion, they stand for violation of law and order.

In the comedy of physical appearances, Falstaff's enormous girth, which invites Hal's merciless comments (357-61), provides much fun. "Bare-bone" Falstaff, Hal suggests, has been blown up by bombast, implying that the old man is devoid of real substance. There is, perhaps, pathos to be found in Sir John's reply: if he has not been able to see his own knees since he was a youth of Hal's age, once, long ago, he was becomingly slender. And, to be sure, he has his own explanation for his corpulence—"a plague of sighing and grief" has blown him up "like a bladder." We are not allowed to sentimentalize; Falstaff's wit drives away sentimentality.

The subsequent dialogue relating to the fearful opponents of Henry IV is especially revealing of Hal's character. Despite all that Falstaff says to undermine the courage of the young prince, Hal remains nonchalant and (thanks probably to the presence of Falstaff) quite witty. What should come through, especially since Hotspur dominated the previous scene and his character has had an important part in the present one, is that Prince Hal finds no occasion to become voluble and boastful about what he intends to do. News of impending conflict does not drive him beyond the bounds of patience. Deeds, not words, are called for, certainly not advertisement of one's self.

The "play extempore," culminating in Falstaff's brilliant defense of himself and his way of life, is a comic masterpiece. Sir

John's genius is fully revealed here as he throws his considerable self into the role of an irate father and king reproving an errant son and heir. He is especially appreciated by the hostess of this disreputable tavern, whom he calls, in lines of heroic verse, his "sweet . . . tristeful queen." Earlier, attention has been called to Falstaff's rather wide range of knowledge, to the fact that his discourse reflects an education appropriate to a knight of the realm. This aspect of his character is again shown, as when he speaks of "King Cambyses' vein," a reference to the ranting style used by Thomas Preston in the widely popular tragedy *Cambyses*, written some twenty-eight years before *1 Henry IV*. More emphatically, it is shown by Falstaff's matchless burlesque of euphuism, the highly contrived style used in the even more widely popular and influential prose romance *Euphues* (1579), by John Lyly. That style, which for a time was widely imitated, is marked by interminable parallelisms and antitheses, rhetorical questions, maxims, and curious allusions and similes which derive from the *Natural History* of Pliny, classical mythology, and the bestiaries of the Middle Ages. All these stylistic devices Falstaff makes use of in his speech, which includes insulting and even scandalous comments on the royal family. He concludes with words of highest praise for "a virtuous man" with whom the prince keeps company. Ah, yes — now he remembers the name. It is Falstaff. Let Hal "him keep with," the rest banish.

When Hal asks that they exchange roles, Falstaff asks, "Depose me?" And he challenges the prince to match him in gravity and majesty. At this point some will be reminded of Hal's solemn promise to break "through the foul and ugly mists/ Of vapours that did seem to strangle him" (I.ii.225-26). If he is to do so, this king of jesters must be deposed.

Actually, Prince Hal, in the role of his father, makes no attempt to rival Falstaff; he makes use of this change to berate the fat knight as (among other things) "that grey iniquity, . . . that villainous abominable misleader of youth, Falstaff, that old white-bearded Satan" (449-509). Then Falstaff, suddenly serious and dutiful in tone as he plays the role of the young heir to the throne, makes his memorable reply, one that is so eloquent, so appealing that generations of theatergoers and readers have taken Falstaff to their hearts—and uncritically have kept him there, whatever his actions have been or will be. Here indeed is verbal brilliance if any is to be found anywhere in literature, dramatic or nondramatic.

There is fine irony in his first statement: he sees no more harm in Falstaff than he sees in himself. He follows this with an appeal for charity. Falstaff is old, he is white-haired; but let no one say he is a whoremaster! It is the strait-laced Puritan who is tacitly denounced in the reference to sack and sugar, fondness for which Falstaff does not deny. Here one of several biblical references used by the knight in the course of the two *Henry IV* plays serves his purpose. Are Pharaoh's lean kine to be loved? And then the incremental refrain on "Jack Falstaff" serves as the peroration. Banish all the other hangers-on at the Boar's-Head Tavern, but banish not Falstaff—the sweet, the kind, the true, the valiant, if old, Jack Falstaff from the prince's company. "Banish plump Jack, and banish all the world."

The commentator who dares to say a word against Sir John at this point of the action risks the charge of lacking a sense of humor (perhaps the most damning charge that can be made against an individual), with the resultant misunderstanding of Falstaff's worth. And yet he has been established as a glutton, one who is devoted largely to the pleasures of the flesh. As Shakespeare has occasion to say elsewhere, wine, used wisely, is a good companion (*Othello*, II.iii.313). In this play, the evidence is complete: Falstaff uses wine in great excess. Nor are all the references to his grey hairs and white beard necessarily intended to invoke pity. Shakespeare's generation belived that age should bring wisdom and a sense of decorum. Carefree escapades may be amusing, even excusable in youth; but in an older person, one who is a ranking member in a hierarchical society, they cannot be laughed away, despite the fact that the rebel latent in many people applauds Falstaff's defiance of the establishment and the sheer brilliance of his defense.

It is with all this in mind that one must evaluate Hal's one-line response after Falstaff has said, "Banish plump Jack, and banish all the world." Says the prince: "I do, I will." Thus, playing the role of king in this play extempore, the heir-apparent embraces law and order; not for long can life be no more than a holiday for him; he has a sacred obligation to fulfill, one that affects the lives of all Englishmen.

Little explication needs to be added. Understandably Falstaff hopes that Hal will not permit the sheriff to enter his tavern sanctuary. His reply to Hal, who once more accuses him of being "a natural coward," is worth brief comment. "I deny your major," he says (544). Falstaff thus spontaneously uses the vocabulary of formal logic, again displaying the range of his knowledge. Moreover, he is not a *natural* coward, as are Bardolph and Peto; he is a coward on principle, that is, when self-interest and self-preservation are involved. He falls asleep behind the arras, confident that the prince will take care of troublesome people like the sheriff.

There is no need to belabor the point relating to the "intolerable deal of sack" consumed by Falstaff—and still not paid for. By the end of this comic scene, preparations are being made for another enterprise involving Hal and his tavern companions, one that will offer a marked contrast to the Gadshill affair. And we learn that Hal, who had told Falstaff that he would not be a thief (I.ii.154) yet had gone along with the rest, will return the money with interest to the travelers.

ACT III—SCENE 1

Summary

In Bangor, Wales, Hotspur and Worcester confer with Glendower, their host, and Mortimer. Young Percy and the Welsh leader, after exchanging compliments, engage in a personal dispute and are interrupted by Mortimer. A map is produced, whereupon the rebel leaders proceed to divide England into three parts—the north going to the Percies, the west to Glendower, and the south to Mortimer. It is Mortimer who explains the immediate action to be taken. He will set forth with Hotspur and Worcester to meet Northumberland and the Scottish forces at Shrewsbury; Glendower, who will need time to muster his forces, will join them later.

Hotspur expresses his dissatisfaction with the division, insisting that the course of the River Trent be changed so as to enlarge his share. Glendower protests, but the two reach an accord.

Mortimer's wife is desolate because her husband must leave her. The couple try to communicate, although neither speaks the other's language. She then sings a Welsh song to the accompaniment of music invoked by Glendower's magic. Hotspur promptly urges his wife to join him in an amorous interlude, and they exchange witty remarks devoid of sentimentality. In short order, however, Hotspur puts an end to this interlude. He will sign the articles of partition and depart for Shrewsbury within two hours.

Commentary

This is the "division" scene; in terms of political doctrine it is especially important. Conceivably some members of Shakespeare's audiences, like many today, had their doubts about the titular hero of this play, Henry IV, recalling not only the illegal manner in which he came to the throne, but also finding him too much the politician, too calculating. For them, Falstaff's comic rationalizations of his own actions to some extent parody those of the king. But few, if any, Englishmen would have tolerated even the thought of division of their country. Their sympathies inevitably would have been on the side of the Crown. Therefore, however valid any complaint by the Percies may have been, their present action, in which they are joined by Mortimer and

Glendower, cannot be justified. In opposing them, the king and his son will emerge as saviors of England.

Fortunately, the heavily doctrinal elements here and elsewhere in the play are rendered sufficiently palatable, thanks largely to superior character portrayal. Not only does Hotspur continue to attract, especially because one sees him in contrast to Prince Hal, but others, including Glendower and Mortimer, interest reader and audience alike. Glendower, it may be noted, is anything but the wild, barbaric figure of the prose histories. And, of course, the scene includes a delightful romantic interlude with music.

Appropriately, it is the character of Hotspur which receives greatest attention in this scene, and his very first speech is revealing. One may question the ultimate worth of a leader who, even momentarily, cannot recall whether he has forgotten or mislaid the important map. This would suggest that he is hardly the one for planning an action, however capable he may be in other areas. Most serious is young Percy's absolute inability to restrain himself, or to tolerate what he considers to be conceit and superstition in Glendower, his host and ally and a man of genuine military greatness. Well along in this scene, Worcester lectures his headstrong nephew, and his words are weighty with import:

> In faith, my lord, you are too wilful-blame;
> And since your coming hither have done enough
> To put him [Glendower] quite beside his patience.
> You must needs learn, lord, to amend this fault.
> Though sometimes it show greatness, courage, blood, —
> And that's the dearest grace it renders you, —
> Yet oftentimes it doth present harsh rage,
> Defect of manners, want of government,
> Pride, haughtiness, opinion and disdain;
> The least of which haunting a nobleman
> Loseth men's hearts and leaves behind a stain
> Upon the beauty of all parts besides,
> Beguiling them of commendation.
>
> (177-89)

"Loseth men's hearts": one recalls that, in the previous scene, Prince Hal had been winning men's hearts!

This is not to say that Hotspur loses one's sympathy in this scene. Quite the contrary. There is graciousness and good heartedness in his reply to his uncle: "Well, I am school'd. Good manners be your speed!" The reader enjoys his satiric thrusts, well illustrated by his reply to Glendower, who claims the ability to "call spirits from the vasty deep":

> Why, so can I, or so can any man;
> But will they come when you do call for them?
>
> (54-55)

Young Percy is no less amusing, but just as tactless and intolerant, when he comments on "lovely English ditties" and Welsh airs and what he calls "mincing poetry." These cultivated subjects have no place in the life of the Hotspur of the North. Although at one point Lady Percy says that her husband is "governed by humours" (237), it is really the single humour insisted upon by Prince Hal in the previous scene which rules him. Compared to either Mortimer or Glendower, whose cultural as well as military accomplishments receive attention, Hotspur is a personable barbarian. It may be added that, although Glendower probably would have had serious difficulty in calling up devils from the vasty deep, Shakespeare does give some evidence of his supernatural powers; for it is Glendower who magically provides the music for the Welsh love song. But, admittedly, the dramatist introduces this rather casually; perhaps, like Hotspur, we are not much impressed.

Something more can be said to the credit of Hotspur. As in Act II, Scene iii, his relation with the lovely Lady Kate, who affectionately calls him a "giddy goose" (232), is delightful. Hotspur's bluffness, his boyish attractiveness comes through strongly. Moreover, gallantry and fair-mindedness remain prominent in his character. When Glendower agrees that the Trent must be "turn'd," Hotspur replies:

I do not care. I'll give thrice so much land
To any well-deserving friend.

(137-38)

ACT III – SCENE 2

Summary

At the palace in London, Prince Hal appears before his father, who dismisses members of his court so that he can speak alone to his son. He passionately censures the heir-apparent for "inordinate and low desires" and for indulging in "such barren pleasures" in the company of such "rude" individuals (12-14), ignoring his status and obligations as a prince. The king seems to believe that Hal's dereliction may be evidence of God's punishment for "some displeasing service" he (the king) has done. Hal does not claim to be blameless, but he states that busybodies and scandalmongers have exaggerated accounts of his behavior.

The king voices his deep concern at considerable length. Hal has absented himself from councils of state, letting his younger brother take his place. If the king himself had chosen, as Hal has done, to cheapen himself in "vulgar company," he never would have won the allegiance of Englishmen. He especially sees in his son the same fatal weaknesses which led to Richard II's downfall. At that time, the king himself was like young Percy, who, no older than Prince Hal, commands "ancient lords and reverend bishops" into battle and has won "never-dying honour" by capturing the renowned Douglas. To Henry IV it seems that Hal is his greatest enemy, not the Northern rebels and Mortimer.

Chagrined by this strong reproof, Prince Hal urges his father not to believe those who have led the king to misjudge him. He solemnly promises to "redeem all this on Percy's head" (132); that is, he will prove his loyalty and worth by performing glorious deeds in opposition to the valiant Hotspur.

Overjoyed, the king declares that Hal will be placed in command of royal forces. The king himself, joined by Westmoreland

and Prince John, will lead another army which will join Hal's in the North.

Sir Walter Blunt arrives with the news that Douglas and the English rebels even now have assembled their troops at Shrewsbury.

Commentary

In this scene the climax and turning point are reached. Because of Hal's vow and his appointment as supreme commander of one large force, the way is prepared also for the shift in the comic subplot. The thematic relationship between main plot and subplot is sufficiently clear, for the reader has come directly from the scene in which this meeting between prince and king has been parodied.

To some, King Henry may appear especially calculating in parts of this scene. Why, for example, should he say to his son:

> I know not whether God will have it so,
> For some displeasing service I have done,
> That, in his secret doom, out of my blood
> He'll breed revengement and a scourge for me.
>
> (4-7)

Perhaps, it is argued, he is not sure that Hal's apparent failure is a sign of God's displeasure; but he is well aware of the "displeasing service" he himself had done — usurpation and regicide. Moreover, his second and much longer speech (29-91) is practical instruction on how to influence people — the right people — what with his remarks on dressing himself "in such humility that [he] did pluck allegiance from men's hearts" (51-52). The point of view represented here is surely not to be ignored, but it may do Henry IV less than justice.

In the first place, it is primarily Henry IV, upholder of law and order, not Henry the sinner, who appears here and in the rest of the play — quite logically, since increasing attention has been paid and will be paid to the rebels. He is the man who, unlike his unfortunate predecessor, is gifted with the arts of kingship. If indeed, according to sixteenth-century political philosophy, the ruler was God's lieutenant on earth, responsible ultimately only to God, he nevertheless must "pluck allegiance from men's hearts," which means that he must win their respect and hold it if his reign is to be successful; after all, God helps them that help themselves. The many contemporary discussions of kingship made all this abundantly clear. The king and father has heard only scandalous reports about his son's behavior. His concern about the succession to the throne is deep and proper; it was a dominant concern of Shakespeare's generation in an England ruled by the Virgin Queen.

Most emphatically now, Prince Hal is pitted against Hotspur. Earlier young Percy had been praised by the king as the "theme of honour's tongue" (I.i.81); now he is "Mars in swathling clothes" (112), a youth no older than Hal who leads high-ranking subjects (a reference to Northumberland, Mortimer, and the Archbishop of York, who are all mentioned in lines 118-19), and who defeated the great Douglas.

At the end of Act I, Scene ii, Hal promised to redeem his tarnished reputation, but he spoke in soliloquy, voicing his secret thoughts, as it were. Now he makes his pledge directly to his king and father. This is not the casual, debonair Prince Hal of the Boar's-Head Tavern speaking. His father's words have penetrated deeply. The very simplicity of his first line underscores his sincerity and determination: "Do not think so; you shall not find it so. . . . (129). He takes his oath "in the name of God" (153). Most readers share the king's elation: "A hundred thousand rebels die in this" (160).

ACT III – SCENE 3

Summary

Falstaff deplores his alleged physical decline resulting from lack of activity since the Gadshill "action." Bardolph's frank comment on the knight's corpulence leads him to a rhetorical exercise, the subject of which is Bardolph's flaming nose. When Mistress Quickly enters, Sir John accuses her of having picked his pockets and he refuses to pay his bill for wine, food, and even items of clothing. The hostess has occasion to mention the prince, whereupon Falstaff calls him a "Jack" (knave) and declares that he would cudgel him if he were present.

The prince enters, marching with Peto. Falstaff joins them, playing on his truncheon (a short staff) as if it were a fife. Falstaff then renews his altercation with the hostess, but when Hal tells him that *he* directed the search of Sir John's pockets, the old knight magnanimously forgives her.

Falstaff is much relieved to learn that all matters relating to the robbery have been settled. Yet the news of Hal's reconciliation with the king hardly elates him, particularly when he is told that he is to command foot soldiers. A serious Prince Hal then gives orders to Bardolph, Peto, and Falstaff, all relating to their services in opposing the rebels.

Commentary

Falstaff's reference to "this last action," a term commonly used for military activity, serves to remind the reader of the connection between the comic subplot and the main plot in this chronicle-history play. One hardly needs the testimony of Bardolph to know that Falstaff has not "dwindled," not "fallen away," either physically or mentally. He is his redoubtable self. His answer to his own questions which begin this scene, complete with witty similes ("like an old lady's loose gown . . . like an old apple-john") tells us as much. Like an old apple, he keeps his flavor; unlike it, he is not shrivelled. We have seen him before in a mood of apparent repentance like the one which follows and are not at all surprised to hear him attribute his fallen state to "company, villainous company", no more than we are surprised to witness the sudden revival of his spirits, thanks to his recourse to hedonist philosophy. When Bardolph remarks that he cannot live long, Sir John replies: "Why, there is it. Come sing me a bawdy song; make me merry" (15-16).

But it is his brilliant comments on Bardolph's physical appearance (27-59) which dominate the first part of this scene. This is an unsurpassed example of the comedy of physical appearance and of words — more specifically the "comedy of noses" (See Rostand's *Cyrano de Bergerac*, wherein the titular hero expounds wittily on the subject of his own nose). To put it another way, this is a comic aria, a bravura piece, all action stopping to give the performer his special opportunity to demonstrate his virtuosity. His evoking of the image of hell's fire (and making another accurate biblical reference) is especially effective; at this point he sounds like a zealous preacher putting the fear of the Lord into the hearts of his listeners.

One additional point may be added. Falstaff has provided the wine for Bardolph for some thirty-two years, we are told (51-55). The time element, probably exaggerated to add to the fun, is not applicable, but the Falstaff of this play has depended upon Hal for the same courtesy. Thus the parasitical aspect of his character again receives notice. As a matter of fact, the interlude involving Mistress Quickly develops this. One learns that the old knight has been victimizing the kindly hostess, who has provided him with drink, food, and clothing.

In this kind of skirmish, or action, be it with the lowly tavern mistress or with the prince himself, Falstaff shows a kind of military genius. His method is to attack; that, quite often, is the best defense. Not irrelevant in this connection is the amusing military pantomine when Hal and Peto march in.

Falstaff is no less accomplished in his responses to the prince. When the hostess reports that Sir John had claimed Hal to be in his debt to the extent of one thousand pounds (a fortune in Shakespeare's day), Falstaff has an unanswerable reply: his love for Hal is worth millions. Nor does he hold the prince in awe, for that emotion is properly to be reserved for the king. He caps all this, tacitly admitting that his pockets had contained only "tavern-reckonings, memorandums of bawdy houses, and one poor penny-worth of sugar-candy" (178-80). He reminds Hal that Adam, progenitor of the human race, fell from a state of innocence, proving that all flesh is weak—and does not he, Falstaff, have more flesh than any other man? Clearly, it will not do to see Falstaff as symbolic of Prince Hal's irresponsible youth any more than it will to reduce him to a single comic type character. He is uniquely himself.

But that is not to say that his wit absolves him from all faults. His status as privileged jester makes it possible for him to urge Hal to "rob . . . the exchequer" at once, now that the prince is on good terms with the king; to suggest that Hal steal a horse for him so that he will not have to lead his soldiers afoot; and to praise rebels on the grounds that they offend only "the virtues" (205 ff.). But the course of life cannot be determined by the atmosphere of an Eastcheap tavern—not if one is to follow it honorably. Unlike Prince Hal, Falstaff is unwilling to give up life as a long series of holidays, even though the fate of the nation is at stake. Quite in character, then, he has his own way of applauding the prince's stirring call to arms ("The land is burning; Percy stands on high"):

> Rare words! brave world! Hostess, my breakfast, come!
> O, I could wish this tavern were my drum!
>
> (229-30)

His sensitive appetite must be satisfied under all circumstances. And it is suggested that he would like to transfer the tavern to the battlefield. Perhaps, in a metaphorical sense, he will do exactly that.

ACT IV—SCENE 1

Summary

The scene now shifts to the rebel camp near Shrewsbury, where Hotspur, Worcester, and Douglas appear. Young Percy and the Scottish warrior exchange compliments. A messenger arrives with news from the Earl of Northumberland. It seems that Hotspur's father is ill and cannot lead his followers to Shrewsbury. Shocked to hear this, Hotspur quickly recovers himself and finds reasons to remain confident: it would be bad strategy to risk his strength in a single encounter; moreover, a victory by the reduced rebel army will redound all the more to their credit, helping to convince the populace at large that the revolt will be successful. Douglas readily endorses these opinions.

Sir Richard Vernon brings news concerning the royal forces. The Earl of Westmoreland and Prince John lead seven thousand soldiers toward Shrewsbury, and the king himself has set forth with another army. Hotspur remains undaunted; he welcomes the opportunity of opposing the royal power. But what, he asks, of Prince Hal? Where is he? Vernon then describes the young heir-apparent "all furnish'd, all in arms," also headed toward the field of battle. Hotspur interrupts Vernon; he cannot bear to hear such words of praise about his royal contemporary. Nevertheless, he now can hardly restrain himself, so anxious is he for the conflict to begin.

There is more news. Vernon reports that Glendower needs more time to muster his power. Worcester and even the fearless Douglas concede that this is the worst news of all. Not Hotspur. When Vernon tells him that the royal forces number 30,000, he exclaims: "Forty let it be!" Douglas joins him in challenging death itself.

Commentary

Although the Battle of Shrewsbury is yet to be fought, the action in the main plot, having reached its climax in Act III, Scene ii, is now falling, structurally speaking. The fortunes of the Percies have been in the ascendent prior to this scene. Now the three items of intelligence mark the turn toward adversity: neither Northumberland nor Glendower will appear with their troops to join those led by Hotspur; the Prince of Wales, having done no more than voice his good intentions, is now acting positively.

The Hotspur in this scene is something more than the limited individual who deserved to be the object of Prince Hal's satire in Act II, Scene iv. He emerges as more than the vain, rather boastful (if courageous) warrior. Although the initial exchange between him and the Earl of Douglas may suggest that the Scotsman is young Percy's alter ego, it is Douglas, not Hotspur, who is the exemplar of unreflecting dauntlessness. Perhaps this difference is implicit in the fact that Douglas is hailed for his courage, Hotspur for his honor. But it is explicit in Hotspur's reaction to the adverse reports—the first brought by the messenger, the second and third by Sir Richard Vernon.

When he learns that his father will not arrive because of "inward" illness (an intentionally ambiguous term), young Percy recognizes the extent to which the odds have shifted and momentarily he loses heart: "This sickness doth infect/ The very life-blood of our enterprise" (28-29); it is "a perilous gash, a very limb lopp'd off" (43). But as a leader he knows that he cannot appear daunted. Promptly he recovers himself and advances reasons for complete confidence in the success of the enterprise. And, of course, Douglas can be depended upon to second him. This is equally true of their reaction to the news about Glendower's inability to muster troops in time, although he had assured the Percies that he would not need even fourteen days. Perhaps there is significance in the Scotsman's reply when Hotspur declares that all goes well: "As heart can think," he says (84). Emotion, not intellect, is his guide.

Vernon's description of the Prince of Wales and Hotspur's reaction call for special comment. From the start, these two have been set in opposition to each other. Young Percy is endorsing little more than the public reputation of the prince (who appropriately is never called "Hal" in these serious scenes of the main plot), one which had been held by King Henry prior to the reconciliation, when he, Percy, refers to him as the "nimble-footed madcap . . . that daff'd [thrust] the world aside and bid it pass" (95-97). Up to end of Act III, the prince in this play has completely ignored public responsibility, so far as positive action is concerned.

Vernon's portrait is that of the Ideal Prince, one that might have been depicted in a rich medieval tapestry. The prince and his followers, wearing the ostrich feather, heraldic emblem of the Prince of Wales, are endowed with spirit and ardor. The prince himself is compared to the Roman god Mercury, a tribute to his prowess: certainly vaulting into the saddle with ease when armor-clad is an impressive accomplishment! Superior horsemanship, it may be added, was an essential accomplishment of the ideal Renaissance man.

Now it is Hotspur alone, not he *and* his comrades, who is momentarily crushed by this report of a battle-ready Prince of Wales: "Worse than the sun in March,/ This praise doth nourish agues," he exclaims (111-12). When he recovers himself, his words comprise a challenge for individual trial by arms:

> Harry to Harry shall, hot horse to horse,
> Meet and ne'er part till one drop down a corse.
>
> (122-23)

In a word, the conflict in the main plot is now assuming the characteristics of a medieval tournament, with an admirable centralizing of the action.

ACT IV – SCENE 2

Summary

Falstaff and Bardolph appear on a public road near Coventry, followed by a newly enlisted company of soldiers. Sir John orders Bardolph to replenish his supply of sack and to tell Peto to meet him at the town's end. He dislikes the idea of marching his men through the town in their rags and tatters. Abjectly impoverished, not one of them could pay him, as so many others had, for release from military service. In Falstaff's own words, "No eye hath seen such scarecrows" (41).

Prince Hal and Westmoreland meet him on the road and comment on the poor creatures whom Falstaff leads. The knight remains undisturbed and is philosophical in the face of this criticism. And, for that matter, the prince seems amused rather than indignant. All are to make haste, says Hal, for Percy is already in the field.

Commentary

Sir John Falstaff, knight of the realm and an officially appointed commander of troops, is off to the wars. A new Falstaff, then? Not at all. This latest "action" provides another occasion for plunder, another chance to show what he thinks of "old father antic the law." Well he knows that the soldier must have his provisions; therefore his first concern has to do with a bottle of sack. In his brilliant soliloquy (12-52), he practically boasts of the disreputable means he has employed to fill the ranks of his company. Nor has he spent a farthing to outfit the beggarly creatures. He had been careful to demand in the king's name those men who would, by one means or another, be able to pay for their release. Then, thanks to the cooperation of minor local officials, he filled the ranks with jail birds — which does not mean that any had been guilty of any serious offense, since roving beggars were subject to arrest in sixteenth-century England. And so these ragged specimens of humanity "march wide betwixt the legs as if they had gyves [fetters] on" (43-44). Led by the corpulent, well-fed Falstaff these bare-boned, lowly subjects are a grotesquely incongruous sight, all the more so if one recalls the splendor of the prince and his fellow warriors in their plumes and glittering gold coats, as described by Sir Richard Vernon in the preceding scene. These "pitiful rascals," as the prince calls them, will win no glory, no honor in the wars. In Falstaff's callous words, they are just "food for powder" (72).

If Falstaff remains a speaker of brilliant prose in this scene, his humor now is grim. Here he is not victimizing a tavern hostess or engaging in robbery devoid of physical violence; he is dealing with the lives of his fellow men, but again he is concerned only with personal gain. He remains "as vigilant as a cat to steal cream" (65). Falstaff must be allowed to follow his course with logical consistency. Significantly, the Prince of Wales does not reprove him; he is permitted to proceed on the march to Shrewsbury.

58

ACT IV – SCENE 3

Summary

Worcester and Vernon try to convince Hotspur that the rebel forces should not attack at once. Douglas sides with young Percy. The sound of a trumpet announces a parley, and Sir Walter Blunt enters "with gracious offers from the king." This gives Hotspur the occasion to review the story of how Henry was helped by the Percies when he returned from exile and how he then usurped the throne. Now, says the young rebel commander, Henry has proved ungrateful to his benefactors and has ignored the proper claims of Mortimer. When Blunt asks if this is Percy's final answer, he is told that it is not. In the morning Hotspur will send Worcester to hear the king's terms and to present their own.

Commentary

The Hotspur of this scene is admirable; he is anything but the foolhardy, impetuous youth. As supreme commander of the rebel forces, he reasons well. Already facing a numerically superior power, he knows that the odds against him will increase unless he commits his troops immediately. In his recital of grievances he invites understanding and sympathy. He expresses a willingness to negotiate if the terms are honorable. The scene thus ends on at least a faint note of hope.

ACT IV – SCENE 4

Summary

The Archbishop of York instructs Sir Michael to deliver in all haste certain written instructions and information to his allies and relatives who have a substantial number of followers. The archbishop has learned that Hotspur faces the king's power without the support of Northumberland, Glendower, and Mortimer. Convinced that young Percy will be defeated, he knows that the king will then move against him for his part in the conspiracy.

Commentary

The consensus is that this scene is to be justified solely on the grounds that it looks forward to the main action in *2 Henry IV*, wherein royal forces indeed move against the archbishop and Lord Mowbray, his most powerful and dependable ally. Yet there is some reason for its inclusion here strictly with reference to *1 Henry IV*. It provides Shakespeare with the opportunity to summarize major events, to foreshadow the rebels' defeat, and to emphasize the seriousness and magnitude of the entire action.

The Sir Michael of this scene does not find a place in history. He may well be a priest, since priests often were given the courtesy title of "Sir."

ACT V – SCENE 1

Summary

The Earl of Worcester and Sir Richard Vernon arrive as emissaries at the king's camp near Shrewsbury. Present are the king himself, the Prince of Wales, John of Lancaster, the Earl of Westmoreland, Sir Walter Blunt, and Falstaff. As Hotspur did earlier in his reply to the king's emissary (IV.iii), Worcester voices at some length the grievances of the Percies, chief of which is Henry's alleged perfidy when, returning from exile, he assured them that he sought no more than the restoration of confiscated Lancastrian estates. The king does not deign to answer this charge; instead he dismisses it as no more than a pretext for rebellion against the Crown. He refuses to permit the Prince of Wales to settle the dispute in single combat with Hotspur. Instead, he offers the rebels free pardon if they will lay down their arms. After Worcester and Vernon leave, the prince states that both Hotspur and Douglas, supremely confident and proven warriors, will reject the offer. The king agrees and orders all officers to their posts.

Falstaff shows little desire to risk his life in any kind of conflict. He asks Hal to keep an eye on him and to help him if necessary. Alone he soliloquizes on the subject of honor and finds no profit in being a dead hero.

Commentary

The opening lines help establish the mood of this scene, the action of which takes place not long before the battle starts. There is rather obvious irony in the speeches of both Worcester and the king. The former makes much of Henry's violation of an oath to the effect that he sought only redress of grievances and not the throne of England, implying that the Percies had no intention of becoming traitors to Richard II. But the reader will recall Hotspur's words spoken early in the play. Northumberland and Worcester "wear the detested blot/ Of murderous subornation . . . Being the agents or base second means,/ The cords, the ladder, or the hangman rather" who made possible the crowning of Henry (I.iii.162 ff.). His solicitude for the fallen Richard, coming so tardily, does not conceal the basic selfish motives of the House of Percy.

It is no less evident that Henry, not content with retrieving the confiscated Lancastrian estates, was strongly motivated by self-interest, specifically, with ambitions toward the throne. But the overwhelming fact now is that he is England's king and has not been guilty of gross misrule as was his predecessor. He is in the process of suppressing "pell mell havoc and confusion"; he seeks to restore law and order in England. If one keeps in mind the view that, in the larger sense, the State is the greater protagonist in the chronicle-history plays, there is a logic here.

Some commentators see calculation in the king's refusal to let his son meet Hotspur in single combat, arguing that Henry is too adroit to take a risk of this sort when he has numerical superiority. Certainly such a conjecture is admissible, but there is also the fact that the demands of recorded history weigh upon the playwright: a Battle of Shrewsbury *must* be fought.

Prince Hal's demeanor is admirable. His offer to meet the renowned Hotspur in single combat is motivated not by a desire to win personal glory but the wish to save lives. His gracious, magnanimous praise of young Percy (85-93) is in the best chivalric tradition, and there is not a hint of false modesty in the deprecatory remarks he makes about himself. Calmly he accepts the fact that death is a constant of armed conflict; he knows that he, like all mortals, "owest God a death" and he will not seek to postpone payment.

Not so Falstaff. Yet his soliloquy on honor, as he conceives it, is a thought-provoking piece in which he develops his theme with such telling particulars that one's immediate reaction may be to endorse his view wholeheartedly. As much as any of his speeches, this one illustrates his wit and verbal skill. Nor can one logically deny the major premise upon which his argument is based. For at the personal level, the utter pathos, even futility, of all armed conflict is exposed. But note that it is the strictly personal, the individual, which concerns Falstaff. Thus, this gifted comic presents at best a half-truth, and perhaps not even that if one recalls this same knight's bland unconcern about the lives of the poor wretches whom he recruited to fight for king and country.

There have been many references to honor in this play: Hotspur's concept of honor to be won and held largely in warfare; Hal's concept, not explicitly defined, but implicit in his burlesque of Hotspur (II.iv), and in the restrained way in which he vowed to make young Percy his "factor" (III.ii). Now Falstaff, who in the comic scenes found occasions to speak of his valor, has given us his concept of honor, one based on self-interest to the exclusion of all else.

ACT V – SCENE 2

Summary

Back in the rebel camp, Worcester insists that Hotspur must not be told that the king has offered all of the insurgents free pardon. He argues that, although his young nephew's trespass will be forgiven, Henry IV will never place his trust in the elder leaders of the rebellion. Vernon reluctantly agrees to remain silent. Accordingly, Worcester tells Hotspur that the king is merciless. Like Douglas, the youth is ready to fight.

When Worcester then tells Hotspur that the prince has challenged him to single combat, the young rebel fervently expresses his wish that such a meeting could take place. He remains skeptical regarding the worth of the prince, even though Vernon describes the latter's chivalric behavior and becoming modesty.

Learning that even now the "King comes on apace," Hotspur exhorts his companions to fight nobly, and then he embraces them as the trumpets sound the start of the conflict.

Commentary

Worcester's decision to keep from Hotspur the "liberal and kind offer of the King" (2) is wholly dishonorable, a monstrous act of treachery against his own flesh and blood, against the unselfish, if misguided, youth who has risen to the position of supreme commander of the insurgents. It is not by mere chance that this episode immediately follows Falstaff's soliloquy on honor. In comparsion to Sir John, the Earl of Worcester is high in the baronial ranks of England; his is an act of betrayal on the grand scale. If the reader has been tempted to accept Falstaff's view of honor as realistic and eminently practical, he may find occasion now to reassess that view. Even in terms of self-interest, Worcester's act of infamy will prove to be impractical.

Vernon's agreeing to go along with Worcester is disappointing, for he has earned the reader's respect and sympathy by his chivalrous conduct. Indeed he does so in this scene by making the generous report of Hal's demeanor (52-69). He too will pay a great price for his compliance.

The character of the Prince of Wales continues to be elevated, thanks to the testimony of Sir Richard Vernon — the testimony of a hostile witness, as it were. The prince's claim made to his royal father, namely, that he had been maligned

(III.iii.130-31) is supported here. Vernon states that the prince has been the victim of envy, or malice, and will be England's "sweet hope" — that is, the Ideal Prince — if his true character is revealed to all.

But the elevation of the prince is not achieved by the denigration of Hotspur's character. If young Percy finds it hard to accept Vernon's flattering description of the prince, he makes use of no term of contempt for his royal rival. In appropriate lines, Percy's courage and honor, as he conceives it, make him an attractive and a worthy opponent. Aware as the reader is that the Percy forces are outnumbered, Hotspur's brief but stirring battle oration (93-101) and his embrace of his fated companions elicit admiration and sympathy.

ACT V — SCENE 3

Summary

On the battlefield Sir Walter Blunt, wearing armor the same as that of the king, meets Douglas, who has slain the Lord of Stafford, similarly arrayed for the obvious purpose of misleading the foe. Now the Scotsman is convinced that it is Henry IV himself whom he faces, and he demands that Blunt surrender. Sir Walter does not reveal his true identity. The two fight and Blunt is slain.

Hotspur enters, speaking words of high praise to the jubilant Douglas, who believes that now "All's done, all's won" (17). Young Percy recognizes Blunt and disillusions his fellow warrior. Both leave to renew the fight elsewhere.

There is the sound of sudden attack. Then Falstaff appears alone. He finds things quite different from what they had been in London; it is not so easy to get off "shot-free" on the battlefield; he may have to pay the bill, which is a rather steep one. Looking down at the body of Sir Walter Blunt, he finds new reason to believe that seeking honor has its grave limitations. From his soliloquy, it is learned that he led his ragged "troops" into the heart of battle and that all but two or three have been slaughtered.

Now it is the prince who arrives. His mood of complete seriousness and dedication to duty is established at once, as he sternly rebukes Falstaff for idleness and asks for the use of his sword. Falstaff boasts about his alleged valor and even claims to have taken care of Hotspur. When Hal assures him that the young rebel survives to slay Falstaff, the fat knight refuses to relinquish his sword, but offers to give Hal his pistol. It is a bottle of sack, not a weapon, which he draws from the case. Hal seizes it, strongly reproves Falstaff, and throws the bottle at him.

Alone once more, Falstaff declares that he will slay Percy if that fearsome enemy survives. But he makes it clear that he is not about to go out of his way to find such "grinning honour" as that possessed by the dead Sir Walter Blunt. Clearly, Hotspur will survive to old age as far as Falstaff is concerned.

Commentary

The report of Douglas' slaying of the Lord of Stafford, his actual slaying of Sir Walter Blunt, and Hotspur's report that the insurgents "stand full fairly for the day" have the important effect of at least equalizing matters relating to the two opposing forces, despite the fact that the royalists outnumber the rebels. In other words, suspense is sustained; it is still touch and go.

Nothing could be much more incongruous, more grotesque, than the appearance of the corpulent, white-bearded, unheroic Falstaff on the battlefield. His brash claims to valor, which are at one with those made in the Boar's-Head Tavern after the Gadshill affair, his irrepressible verbal wit ("Ay, Hal; 'tis hot,'tis hot./ There's that will sack a city.") provide a counterbalance to the heroics in this scene, which, by themselves, might well be given such emphasis as to be a bit ludicrous — excessively melodramatic in dramatic fiction.

Falstaff *has*, in a metaphorical sense, brought the tavern to the battlefield. The bottle of sack, in place of the pistol in the case, is emblematic. The braggart warrior, one of the facets of his complex character, finds expression here when he assures the prince that "Turk Gregory" never matched his deeds in arms. The allusion, in all probability, is to Pope Gregory VII, noted for ferocity, here given the title of "Turk" since the Turks were held to be exemplars of cruelty.

Now in the midst of battle, the prince has no occasion to indulge in the slightest witticism in his exchange with Falstaff. Sternly he rebukes Sir John: "What, is it a time to jest and dally now?" (57). Certainly the knight's sense of timing is lamentably bad.

ACT V – SCENE 4

Summary

The king bids the Prince of Wales and his brother, John of Lancaster, to rest. Despite his wounds, the prince will not do so: ". . . God forbid a shallow scratch should drive/ The Prince of Wales from such a field as this,/ Where . . . rebels' arms triumph in massacres" (11-14). He has high praise for his younger brother, whose courage inspires them all. The two depart.

Douglas enters, faces Henry IV, and exclaims: "Another king!" He identifies himself and demands to know the true identity of his foe. The king expresses his regret that, until now, the Scottish warrior has met only "his shadows" — nobles whom he mistook for the king. While his son seeks out Percy, Henry will take on Douglas.

The king is in danger of defeat when Prince Hal enters. The latter identifies himself as the heir-apparent, engages Douglas in single combat, and forces his adversary to flee for his life. King Henry is particularly touched by this evidence of his son's courage.

After the king leaves, Hotspur enters, addresses the prince by name and identifies himself. Now at last Harry *does* meet Harry face to face in combat. Falstaff appears to cheer Prince Hal, who will, as he says, "find no boy's play here" (76). At this point in the action, Douglas re-enters and engages Falstaff, who soon falls down as if he were dead. Just as Douglas leaves, Hotspur himself is wounded and falls.

In moving words, young Percy begins to recite his own epitaph but dies before he can finish. It is the prince who, in generous terms, completes it.

The prince sees the fallen Sir John Falstaff. Believing his old companion to be dead (if one takes his words literally), he now provides an epitaph for "Poor Jack," referring to him as "so fat a deer" and declaring that he will see him "embowell'd" (103-10). Hal departs.

Falstaff promptly revives and rises up. As in earlier, far less serious, episodes, he indulges in witty rationalization for his unheroic behavior—specifically, in this case, counterfeiting death. Next, he expresses his fear of "this gunpowder Percy," who is apparently dead. Perhaps, he says, young Percy is "counterfeiting" as Falstaff himself did. He decides to "make him sure"—and then to claim that it was he who killed the valiant rebel leader. No living person is nearby to see him; so he stabs the corpse of the fallen Hotspur. He lifts the body onto his back just as Prince Hal and John of Lancaster re-enter.

Prince John is puzzled: did not Hal tell him that the old knight had been killed? Hal replies that indeed he saw Falstaff "dead,/ Breathless and bleeding on the ground" (137). Sir John, he concludes, is not what he seems.

Indeed he is not, replies Falstaff. As conqueror of the great Percy, he looks to be made either an earl or a duke. He is deeply shocked to hear the prince claim to have slain Hotspur. Prince Hal is not perturbed; he is not concerned with refuting Sir John. As he says to his brother, if a lie will serve Falstaff, he will not interfere.

A trumpet sounds retreat. All know that the rebels have been defeated. The two princes leave to find out how their comrades have fared. Falstaff will follow—for his reward, as he makes clear.

Commentary

Although another scene follows, this one provides the essential resolution of the action. From the start, the character of Prince Hal is enhanced. He refuses to leave the battlefield, despite his wounds; he demonstrates at once his humility and his magnanimity in praising the deeds performed by his younger brother. Even more impressive is the fact that he saves the life of Henry IV, exponent and symbol of law and order in the realm. That the father should be deeply touched comes as something of a surprise. He had distrusted his son, believing that Hal wanted him to die. Now the reader knows how malicious indeed were the slanders against the spirited young prince who had chosen to play the truant for a while.

Although the battle necessarily is presented in a series of separate episodes, the encounter between Prince Hal and Hotspur is the climactic one, for it conveys the impression that the prince's triumph ended the conflict. It will be recalled that Douglas, believing that he had slain the king, was convinced that his action meant total victory for the rebels. Young Percy was the leader of the insurgents.

Hotspur, whose high courage and gallantry have received increasing emphasis, invites one's whole-hearted sympathy as he falls before the prince's sword; his indeed was "a great heart." Surely no one would care to gloat over the fact that this same Hotspur had spoken contemptuously of Hal, refusing to believe that the prince was capable of serious action. For one thing, it was not life *per se* but his matchless reputation as a great warrior which concerned him most. Nor does this suggest undue vanity. He had been no braggart warrior; his titles had been won honestly. Like other dying great men elsewhere in Shakespeare, but perhaps unexpected in this heretofore unreflecting young soldier, Hotspur philosophizes in almost a medieval fashion, seeing himself as "time's fool." Those near death were thought to have the gift of prophecy; Hotspur, had he time, could prophesy. What could he foresee? Unquestionably the triumph of Henry V over the numerically superior French — the emergence of Prince Hal as hero-king of England. Just as Hotspur's courage, sense of honor, and gallantry were stressed increasingly in the later scenes, so Prince Hal's pre-eminence is emphasized. Young Percy has been established fully as the most worthy of all opponents; his conqueror emerges as a completely heroic figure, one almost larger than life itself. Appropriately, there is no suggestion of personal triumph in Hal's words. Magnaminity determines their tone, for he dwells upon young Percy's knightly virtues, his breadth of spirit, the high respect merited by one of such "great heart."

If valid military honor is the subject of this episode, the Falstaffian one which follows provides a grimly comic exercise on bogus military honor. When Hal sees Falstaff lying on the battlefield, he has a valediction for him, one no less appropriate than the one for Hotspur. The prince's statement that he could have "spar'd a better man" (104) probably is purposely ambiguous. For holidays, those occasional times when care may be put aside, there is no better man than Falstaff in the sense of being more entertaining. But life, certainly for the heir to the throne, cannot remain a perpetual holiday. It follows that the prince is not so much in love with "vanity" as to be crushed by the end of all that Falstaff represents.

There is another possibility here. "I know you all," the prince soliloquized at the end of Act I, Scene i; and his remarks to and concerning Falstaff throughout the play have left no doubt that he does fully understand his amusing companion. With this in mind, it may be argued that he is fully aware now that Falstaff is up to his old tricks again. Perhaps his play on the words *heavy* ("O, I should have a heavy miss of thee") and *deer* ("so fat a deer") and the reference to "embowelling," may well be taken as an indication that Hal knows Falstaff hears every word spoken. But admittedly all this is conjecture.

The Gadshill episode established the fact that Falstaff was a coward on principle, not a born coward like Peto or Bardolph. So he is here, as his famous line, "The better part of valour is discretion; in the which better part I have saved my life"

(120-22), makes clear. To be sure, there is an important element of truth in what he says, just as there was in his comments on honor. But there is also a cynical perversion of an abiding truth. Young Percy, prior to the Battle of Shrewsbury, well could have employed discretion without sacrifice of valor, for he was far above self-centered consideration. Discretion to Falstaff means self-preservation and no more.

There was sufficient falling off in the character of Falstaff, with reference to his recruits; there is more now. Sir John Falstaff, knight of the realm, stabs the fallen Hotspur in the thigh, an act which involves complete renunciation of the chivalric code. It is an act of monstrous desecration, absolutely inexcusable.

One may presume that he no more expects to be believed when he claims to have slain Hotspur than he had expected Hal and Poins to believe his story of what happened at Gadshill, for one cannot deprive the witty, knowledgeable Falstaff of ordinary common sense. Hal had tricked him there; now he tricks Hal. And, if on principle he is cowardly where physical action is involved, in the realm of rhetoric he is dauntless. "There is Percy," he exclaims, throwing the body to the earth (142)—a salvo defying refutation. With the same confidence, he expects great reward. At the end of this scene, he says: "I'll follow, as they say, for reward. He that rewards me, God reward him" (166-67). That too has been a great part of his life's philosophy; throughout the play he has followed for reward.

But Falstaff will not permit us to dismiss him scornfully, for his superior wit never deserts him and, in a sense, he has considerable capacity for self-criticism. The thought strikes him that, should he be elevated to a dukedom, actually he will "grow less," for such high rank has its obligations: the king of jesters would have to abdicate.

One other point relating to Falstaff's conduct needs to be settled. Those who refuse to find any fault in this man, who is to them the true hero of this play, make much of his statement that he led his men into the heart of battle. This, it is argued, is irrefutable proof of his personal valor. But is it? Did he actually place himself at the head of his company when he committed it to battle? And did he then, thanks to great martial prowess, survive without a scratch despite his enormous girth? In the next episode he counterfeits death as a means of escaping once more "shot free." Perhaps that was not the first time in which he employed the ruse. Certainly Elizabethans would not interpret the word "led" as proof of Falstaff's courage—not in view of the frequent charges made against leaders who committed their troops to battle but avoided danger themselves. These charges may well provide a revealing insight into Falstaff's actions—and may be at one with his having "misused the king's press damnably" in recruiting his soldiers.

Prince Hal deserves the last word. His superiority and his magnanimity are well illustrated by his refusal to argue with Falstaff or to show the slightest concern about being deprived of the credit for the defeat of a great adversary. He is quite willing to humor this knight of the "latter spring." Nevertheless, it is worth noting that, since Shakespeare indubitably had the sequel to this play in mind, Falstaff cannot be rejected at the end of *1 Henry IV*.

ACT V—SCENE 5

Summary

The insurrection having been repressed, King Henry orders the execution of Worcester and Vernon. The fate of the other rebels will be decided later. Prince Hal intercedes on behalf of the Earl of Douglas, and his life is spared. Prince John of Lancaster is given the honor of setting the Scotsman free. The king then announces that he will divide his forces. One army, led by Prince John and the Earl of Westmoreland, will move against the forces assembled by Northumberland and Archbishop Scroop in northern England. Accompanied by Prince Hal, Henry himself will march to Wales to fight Glendower and Mortimer.

Commentary

"Thus ever did rebellion find rebuke." This opening line, spoken by the titular hero, summarizes the major theme of the play. Another line spoken by the king at the end of this scene points to the theme of 2 *Henry IV:* "Rebellion in this land shall lose its sway" (41).

Henry's strong words indicting the Earl of Worcester serve a two-fold purpose. First and most important, these leave the impression at the end of the play that Henry IV is a strong, yet fair-minded ruler, one who gave the rebels every chance to embrace law and order before he moved against them. Second, if a villain is to be found in the main plot, he must be Worcester, who was largely responsible for schooling young Percy and who, as Henry reminds him, had not borne "true intelligence" from the king to the other rebel leaders at Shrewsbury.

Hal now is the Ideal Prince. Properly, it is he who saves the life of the "noble Scot, Lord Douglas" and who delegates to John of Lancaster the "high honour" of freeing Douglas without ransom. Since Vernon has been depicted as no less noble and admirable, one may question why the prince's generosity did not extend to him. It is to be remembered, however, that Douglas, a valiant foe, is not an Englishman, not a rebel against a king to whom he had sworn allegiance.

MEDIUM: VERSE AND PROSE

Quite properly verse is overwhelmingly the medium used in the main plot, the wholly serious action; no less appropriately prose is used almost entirely in the broadly comic subplot. Of the nineteen scenes, ten are devoted entirely to the serious action, six largely to the comic, and three (wherein Falstaff appears on the battlefield) to a mixture of the serious and the comic. The principle of decorum invariably determines the choice of medium. When Hal speaks as the heir-apparent, he does so in iambic pentameter lines, usually blank verse. Not only is this true when he soliloquizes at the end of the first comic scene (I.ii.218-40), but elsewhere. At the end of Act II, Scene ii, just after he and Poins have confronted Falstaff, Bardolph, and Peto and relieved them of the booty and put them to flight, Hal speaks to Poins in blank verse:

> Got with much ease. Now merrilly to horse.
> The thieves are all scatter'd and possess'd with fear
> So strongly that they dare not meet each other;
> Each takes his fellow for an officer.
> Away, good Ned. Falstaff sweats to death,
> And lards the lean earth as he walks along.
> Were't not for laughing, I should pity him.
>
> (111-17)

One may have his misgivings regarding the morality here, since it is not until later that the prince returns the booty with interest. But it would seem that Shakespeare intends us to understand that the heir-apparent is already giving evidence of his true character, looking forward to the day when he will provide more convincing evidence of his dedication to law and order. Even more appropriate is the prince's shift to verse at the end of Act III, Scene iii, when he is about to leave for the wars. To Falstaff he says:

> There [in Temple Hall] shalt thou know thy charge,
>   and there receive
> Money and order for their furniture.
> The land is burning; Percy stands on high;
> And either we or they must lower lie.
>
> (225-28)

As one reads these measured lines, he knows that, in this play, Hal has said goodbye to the carefree life at Boar's-Head Tavern.

Blank verse belongs especially to the main plot, where the very fate of the realm is the issue. Often it is quite formal, notably an idealization of ordinary discourse. Decorum calls for such verse when King Henry is addressing recalcitrant nobles (Act I,

Scene ii) and when he is addressing his truant son (Act III, Scene ii); it is also used when Sir Walter Blunt, emissary from the king, conveys his important message to the rebel leaders (Act IV, Scene iii). But to compare the blank verse in this play with that, say, of the *Henry VI* plays and *Richard III,* all of which date several years earlier, is to realize how great has been the poet-dramatist's advance, how impressive the mastery of the medium. Not only are some twenty-three percent of the blank verse lines in *1 Henry IV* "run-on" lines (that is, running the sense and grammatical structure past the end of a given line and thus avoiding what has been called "iambic monotony"), but over fourteen percent contain speeches ending within the line. Consider, for example, the following quotation:

> *Wor.* Good cousin, give me audience for a while.
> *Hot.* I cry you mercy.
> *Wor.*   Those same noble Scots
>   That are your prisoners, —
> *Hot.*   I'll keep them all!
>   By God, he shall not have a Scot of them;
>   No, if a Scot would save his soul, he shall not!
>   I'll keep them, by this hand.
> *Wor.*   You start away
>   And lend no ear unto my purposes.
>   Those prisoners you shall keep.
> *Hot.*   Nay, I will; that's flat.
>   (I.iii.211-18)

No one with any sensitivity to rhythm can miss the iambic beat in these lines, which conveys as well as prose possibly could the sense of reality, vivid and dramatic.

Rhymed iambic pentameter couplets occur thirty-two times, usually at the end of speeches and of scenes, for which they provide a particular kind of emphasis, as in these lines:

> *Hot.* Uncle, adieu! O, let the hours be short
>   Till fields and blows and groans applaud our sport!
>   (I.iii.301-2)

> *King.* Our hands are full of business; let's away.
> Advantage feeds him fat, while men delay.
>
> (III.ii.179-80)

> *Hot.* Harry to Harry shall, hot horse to horse,
> Meet and ne'er part till one drop down a corse.
>
> (IV.i.122-23)

By the time he came to write the *Henry IV* plays, Shakespeare habitually used prose for comic scenes, even for high comedy, not solely for broad or "low" comedy. When the comic element is to the fore, Prince Hal and all the others speak prose. Falstaff has already been identified as a speaker of great prose. His discourse has wide range and always reflects his sophistication and wit. His careful use of repetitions, rhetorical questions, apt allusions, balance, and antitheses is remarkable. His burlesque of euphuism, used when he plays the role of Hal's father, provides sufficient evidence that he recognizes the affected, the contrived, and the artificial for what it is. The following quotations will serve, perhaps, to illustrate his skill:

> Marry, then, sweet wag, when thou art king, let not us that are squires of the night's body be called thieves of the day's beauty. Let us be Diana's foresters, gentlemen of the shade, minions of the moon; and let men say we be men of good government, being govern'd, as the sea is, by our noble and chaste mistress the moon, under whose countenance we steal.
>
> (I.ii.26-33)

> But, Hal, I prithee, trouble me no more with vanity. I would to God thou and I knew where a commodity of good names were to be bought. An old lord of the council rated me the other day in the street about you, sir, but I mark'd him not; and yet he talk'd very wisely, but I regarded him not; and yet he talk'd wisely, and in the street too.
>
> (I.ii.83-98)

If first honors belong to Falstaff, it must be acknowledged that Prince Hal exhibits great skill in prose discourse, matching

Sir John similitude for similitude on occasion, as in the following lines:

> *Fal.*   'Sblood, I am
>   as melancholy as a gib cat or a lugg'd bear.
> *Prince.* Or an old lion, or a lover's lute.
> *Fal.* Yea, or the drone of a Lincolnshire bagpipe.
> *Prince.* What sayest thou to a hare, or the melancholy of
>   Moor-ditch?
>
>   (I.ii.82-88)

The prose of both prince and knight provides an interesting contrast to that of the lowly carriers at the beginning of Act II, Scene i — and, for that matter, to the prose used by Gadshill a bit later in the same scene.

The range in kinds of prose may be further illustrated. Hotspur employs a style appropriate to subject, mood, and character in two different scenes: first, when he reads and provides commentary on the letter from the timorous lord whose support he has sought (II.iii.1 ff.); second, in the dialogue with his Lady Kate, the amusing if tactless satire of Mortimer and his Welsh-speaking wife (III.i.241 ff.).

SIXTEENTH-CENTURY POLITICAL THEORY

Since the *Henry IV* plays are basically political ones, it is necessary to understand the political doctrine behind them if one is to do justice to Shakespeare's intentions. Elizabeth I, the fifth Tudor to rule England, had come to a throne which was in many ways insecure because of rival claims. Henry VIII, her father, had found it especially necessary to inculcate the doctrine of absolute obedience to the Crown after the break with Rome in 1536. During his reign he had experienced the Pilgrimage of Grace, a rebellion in northern England, and, later, the Exeter Conspiracy, an alleged attempt to depose Henry and place a Yorkist on the throne of England. After Henry VIII's death,

England endured the Western Rebellion of 1549; during Elizabeth's reign there occurred the Rebellion of 1569, as well as
plots against the queen's life, notably the Babington Plot, which
led to the trial, conviction, and execution of Mary, Queen of
Scots. Throughout the century and beyond, England had reason
to fear an invasion and the rising of native Catholics. The danger
was by no means restricted to the year 1588, when Philip II of
Spain sent his Armada to subdue England.

In view of such challenges to Tudor supremacy, there was a
need for a political philosophy which would prevent challenges
to royal authority and devastating civil war. The basic arguments
were developed during the reign of Henry VIII and augmented
as new crises arose during the reigns of Edward VI and Elizabeth
I. It found expression in officially approved pamphlets and tracts,
and also in drama and non-dramatic poetry. Especially it was
emphasized in official sermons, the first group of which was
introduced in the year 1549. These included strongly worded
instruction on the subject of obedience. They were augmented
in 1570, following the Rebellion of 1569 and the papal decree of
excommunication of Queen Elizabeth I. Every Englishman was
required to hear the sermons on obedience three times during
the year. The gist of the doctrine was this: the ruler was God's
lieutenant on earth; no subject, however exalted, had the right
actively to oppose him. To do so was a sin against religion
punishable by suffering here and now and by eternal damnation
after death. Even if the ruler were a tyrant, the subject had no
right to oppose him; for the head of state ruled with God's suf-
ferance. In support of this doctrine, appeals were made primarily
to biblical authority. Texts such as Romans 13 and Proverbs 8,
as well as ones in Matthew, were cited repeatedly. John of
Gaunt, Duke of Lancaster, summed up the doctrine accurately
and concisely in his response to his sister-in-law, the Duchess
of Gloucester, who reminded him that the reigning king, Richard II, had been responsible for the death of her husband and
Gaunt's brother:

> God's is the quarrel, for God's substitute,
> His deputy anointed in His sight,

Hath caus'd his death; the which if wrongfully,
Let Heaven revenge; for I may never lift
An angry arm against His minister.

(Richard II, I.ii.37-41)

That Henry IV should so suffer is to be explained by the fact that he, son of John of Gaunt, did "lift an angry arm against [God's] minister." He endures rebellion; he sees the apparent waywardness of Prince Hal as part of his punishment; he is not permitted to lead a crusade against the foes of Christianity and do penance for his grievous sins. But, according to Tudor political theory, he wore the crown by God's authority; no subject had the right to oppose him. All this should make understandable the Percies' position and make unacceptable the view that Henry IV is a hypocrite.

REVIEW QUESTIONS

1. In what sense are there *two* kings of England in this play?

2. In terms of debits and credits, what are the chief facets of Falstaff's character?

3. In your opinion what is the chief contribution made respectively by:

    a. Bardolph

    b. Francis

    c. Vernon

4. What are the virtues and the limitations of Hotspur?

5. Hotspur refers to Henry IV as "this vile politician Bolingbroke." What justification does he have for this term?

6. How does the character of Hotspur compare with:

   a. Prince Hal

   b. Douglas

   c. Worcester

7. What do you find especially revealing in these lines as regards theme, plot, or character?

   a. *Falstaff:* O, I could wish this tavern were my drum!
      (III.iii.230)

   b. *Prince Hal:* If all the year were playing holidays,
      To sport would be as tedious as to work;
      But when they seldom come, they wish'd for come,
      And nothing pleaseth but rare accidents.
      (I.ii.227-30)

   c. *King.* A hundred thousand rebels die in this.
      Thou shalt have charge and sovereign trust therein.
      (III.ii.160-61)

8. To whom is reference made and what is the explanation of:

   a. "Mars in swathling clothes" (III.ii)

   b. "thou latter spring!" (I.ii)

   c. "Harry to Harry shall, horse to horse, meet" (IV.i)

   d. "time's fool" (V.iv)

9. What possible relationship is there between:
   a. The planning of the Gadshill robbery and the scenes in which the Percies discuss the revolt against Henry IV?

b. The gulling of Falstaff in Act II and Falstaff's claim to have slain Hotspur in Act V?

10. What excuse is there for the presence of Archbishop Scroop in this play?

SELECTED BIBLIOGRAPHY

Texts

HEMINGWAY, SAMUEL B. (ed.). *Henry the Fourth, Part I.* A New Variorum Edition. Philadelphia: J. B. Lippincott, 1936. Includes text, textual notes, sources, general criticism, stage history, and bibliography.

HUMPHREY, A. R. (ed.). *The First Part of Henry IV.* The Arden Shakespeare. London: Methuen, 1960.

NIELSON, W. A., and C. J. HILL (eds.). *The Complete Plays and Poems of William Shakespeare.* Houghton Mifflin, 1942. The Notes are based on this complete edition of Shakespeare's works.

Bibliographies

BERMAN, RONALD. *A Readers' Guide to Shakespeare's Plays. A Discursive Bibliography.* Chicago: Scott, Foresman, 1965.

Criticism

CAMPBELL, LILY B. *Shakespeare's 'Histories': Mirrors of Elizabethan Policy.* San Marino, California: 1947. Completely sound study of the *Henry IV* plays as exemplars of rebellion.

CHAMBERS, E. K. *William Shakespeare: A Study of Facts and Problems.* 2 vols. Oxford, 1930. Basic to textual study of the play.

DANBY, JOHN. *Shakespeare's Doctrine of Nature*. London: Faber and Faber, 1949. Includes provocative discussion of what the author considers to be the increasingly secular outlook in the chronicle-history plays.

EMPSON, WILLIAM. *Some Versions of Pastoral*. Norfolk, Conn: New Directions, 1950. Includes short but stimulating study of the *Henry IV* plays in which the critic identifies three worlds, each with its own hero: the rebel camp, the tavern, and the court.

PALMER, JOHN. *Political and Comic Characters of Shakespeare*. London: Macmillan, 1962. Good discussion of Falstaff and politics.

TILLYARD, E. M. W. *Shakespeare's History Plays*. London: Chatto and Windus, 1944. Excellent discussion of Prince Hal in particular, relating his character to certain Renaissance values.

TRAVERSI, D. A. *Shakespeare from Richard II to Henry V*. Stanford University Press, 1957. Scene by scene analysis, with particular attention paid to the themes of policy, honor, and retribution.

WILSON, J. D. *The Fortunes of Falstaff*. New York: Macmillan, 1944. Searches for Falstaffian origins in pre-Shakespearean drama; includes a good analysis of Falstaff's character and actions in the *Henry IV* plays.

——. Shakespeare's *Histories at Stratford*. New York: Theatre Art Books, 1952. Warns against over-moralizing in *Henry IV*.